# Introduction

Until recently, there has been a pessimism about the management of chronic obstructive pulmonary disease. A pessimism from clinicians who have been hampered not only by the lack of accessible tools to help with diagnosis, but also by a lack of clarity about the goals of management and how to achieve them, and the paucity of useful therapeutic interventions. A pessimism too from patients who have perhaps failed to come forward, aware of a relative lack of interest in the disease, a sense of personal guilt over the cause – probably cigarette smoking – and fearing the inevitable first intervention: encouragement from health care professionals to stop.

About 900 000 people in the UK have been diagnosed with COPD, around 1.5% of the whole population, so no-one underestimates the scale of the issue and the enormous burden placed on clinicians in both primary and secondary care, and payors. Worldwide, COPD is currently the fifth most common cause of death; it is expected to be the third commonest by 2020, with the greatest burden of disease shifting to developing countries, particularly in the Far East.

Nor will anyone underestimate the impact on patients: daily symptoms, restrictions on daily activities, health care contacts, terrifying exacerbations and disturbing mortality figures.

But perhaps attitudes are now changing. The status of COPD in the new General Medical Services contract for UK General Practitioners has helped to accelerate the attention to the condition in UK primary care. Earlier and more accurate diagnosis offers an opportunity to intervene sooner in the course of the disease. Smoking cessation programmes are better organised and better funded, with a wider range of pharmacological and non-pharmacological support for smokers available. Outcomes in COPD management other than attempting to decrease the rate of lung function decline have been studied, and strategies for improving them have been proposed. Greater collaboration between health care agencies has seen better pulmonary rehabilitation programmes, including attention to diet and exercise, greater availability of domiciliary and portable oxygen and the introduction of 'hospital at home' services. At a political and public health level, radical proposals to ban smoking in public places has both a direct health benefit but also perhaps an indirect benefit by both creating a debate about the causes and effects of smoking and by legitimising and encouraging attempts to stop, or not start, smoking.

The aim of this book is to help primary care clinicians manage COPD at both an individual and practice level and to highlight the roles of other colleagues that patients with COPD might encounter in the management of their disease.

## Contributing authors

**Presentation, diagnosis and differential diagnosis**
Dr Paul Stephenson
and Prof Martyn Partridge

**Pathology of COPD**
Prof Peter Jeffery

**Spirometry: an introduction**
Dr Paul Stephenson and Prof Martyn Partridge

**COPD as a systemic disease**
Dr Mangalam Sridhar

**Smoking cessation**
Jane Scullion

**Exacerbation of COPD in Primary Care**
Dr Rupert Jones

**Management of acute exacerbation in Secondary Care**
Dr Mangalam Sridhar

**Pharmacotherapy of COPD**
Dr John Haughney

**Self management in COPD**
Prof Martyn Partridge

**Pulmonary rehabilitation**
Jane Scullion

**Domicilliary oxygen**
Prof Martyn Partridge

**Investigation of COPD in secondary care and rarer differential diagnosis**
Dr Mangalam Sridhar

**Providing a integrated care service for COPD**
Dr Rupert Jones

**Palliative care in COPD**
Jane Scullion and Dr Rupert Jones

**COPD and the new GMS contract for UK general practice**
Dr John Haughney

## About the authors:

**Dr John Haughney** is a GP in Glasgow and the immediate past chairman of the UK General Practice Airways Group. He is a part time research fellow at the University of Aberdeen and sits on the steering committee of the SIGN / BTS UK asthma guideline.

**Professor Peter Jeffery** is director of Lung Pathology in the Department of Gene Therapy, Imperial College London based at the Royal Brompton Hospital. He specialises in studies of airway biopsies, inflammation and remodelling in COPD and asthma and in the assessment of treatments using pharmacological or gene therapy approaches.

**Dr Rupert Jones** is a Clinical Research Fellow at the Peninsula Medical School, Plymouth, where he leads the Respiratory Research Unit. His research interests include psychological factors in COPD, pulmonary rehabilitation, compliance and self-management.

**Martyn Partridge** is Professor of Respiratory Medicine in Imperial College, London, and Honorary Consultant Physician to Hammersmith Hospitals NHS Trust based at Charing Cross Hospital

**Jane Scullion** is a Respiratory Nurse Consultant  University Hospitals of Leicester and part time Clinical Fellow University of Aberdeen Department of General Practice and Primary Care.

**Dr Managalam Sridhar** is a Consultant Physician and Honorary Senior Lecturer at the Charing Cross site of Hammersmith Hospitals NHS Trust and NHLI Division of Imperial College, London. He was a member of the Consensus Reference Group that contributed to the NICE guideline on COPD.

**Paul Stephenson** is a full-time GP principal in Haverhill, West Suffolk, and is an active member and former committee member of the GPIAG. He is a committee member of the East Anglian Confidential Enquiry into Asthma Deaths and is Deputy Editor of the Primary Care Respiratory Journal.

# Contents

# Chapter **1**

## Presentation, Diagnosis and Differential Diagnosis of Chronic Obstructive Pulmonary Disease

**In this chapter:**

Symptoms of cough and breathlessness are common, and shared with diseases of both the lungs and other systems.

Careful history taking is important.

The information required to make a correct diagnosis of COPD is given.

Diagnostic pitfalls are discussed.

The major symptoms of chronic obstructive pulmonary disease (COPD) are breathlessness and cough. These symptoms are shared not only with many lung diseases, but also with disorders of other systems. For misdiagnosis not to occur, it is essential for clinicians to have a system to ensure that the symptoms of cough and breathlessness are investigated and attributed correctly.

## Risk factors for COPD

Risk factors for COPD can be divided into environmental factors and intrinsic host factors. The major environmental risk factor for COPD is cigarette smoking. It is important to consider the extent of the smoking history. A 'pack year' is the smoking of 20 cigarettes a day for a year: so a patient who has smoked 20 cigarettes/day for 20 years has a smoking history of '20 pack years'; a patient who has smoked 30 cigarettes a day for 1 year has a smoking history of 1.5 pack years; and a patient who has smoked 30 cigarettes a day for 30 years has a smoking history of (30 x 1.5) or 45 pack years. However, not all heavy smokers develop clinically significant COPD, so there must be some genetic modification of risk given the same amount of exposure. In various studies 20–25% and up to 50% of smokers have been reported to develop COPD.

Other environmental factors such as occupational dusts and chemicals, and indoor and outdoor pollutants might need to be considered – though the impact of occupational dusts is dependent on intense and/or very prolonged exposure in order for it to be a risk factor independent of cigarette smoking. The role of outdoor pollution is probably small. Other possible environmental risk factors such as persistent respiratory infections and low socio-economic status have been mooted – but the difficulty would be in isolating these as risk factors in the absence of other more important (and more common) factors.

The major identified intrinsic host risk factor for COPD is homozygous $\alpha$-1 antitrypsin deficiency, which leads to premature and accelerated development of panlobular emphysema. A family history of early COPD, and presentation of symptoms in a relatively young adult, should necessitate consideration of $\alpha$-1 antitrypsin deficiency as a diagnosis.

There is now increasing evidence from long-term longitudinal studies of childhood wheezing illness that one particular phenotype, the 'early wheezers' (whose wheezing is probably caused by slightly abnormal airway architecture either because of lung prematurity at birth or exposure to maternal smoking *in utero*), might well predispose to 'bronchitis' in adult life. A history of recurrent childhood and adolescent respiratory illness, therefore, might well be a further clue in a patient presenting with possible COPD.

## Clinical presentation and initial assessment

COPD can be considered to have two major clinical components: the hyper-secretory disorder which manifests as a cough productive of sputum; and the airway disorder, which manifests as airway narrowing and resultant breathlessness.

Cough is an early symptom to develop in COPD. Initially it may be intermittent, but, as the severity of the disease develops, the cough tends to be more persistent, occurring every day and night.

Chronic sputum production occurs in conjunction with the chronic cough. The old definition of 'chronic bronchitis' – a daily cough with sputum production for 3 months a year for at least two consecutive years – defines the hyper-secretory form of COPD, but any pattern of chronic sputum production can signify COPD.

Breathlessness, which is persistent and progressive, is the reason that most COPD patients seek medical attention and is the major cause of disability in COPD. The dyspnoea is worse on exertion, worse with infections and, as the COPD becomes more severe and lung function reduces, it becomes progressively more obvious and obtrusive.

Taking a good history in the consultation will establish the likelihood of the diagnosis by:

- assessment of various risk factors, in particular the extent of the smoking history ('pack years')
- assessing the symptoms and clinical presentation
- consideration of the possible differential diagnoses.

## Diagnosis and differential diagnosis

A diagnosis of COPD needs to be considered in any patient presenting with per-sistent cough, sputum production and shortness of breath.

Cough may reflect a variety of conditions:

- airway disorders such as asthma, COPD, lung cancer or bronchiectasis
- diffuse parenchymal lung disease, such as asbestosis or fibrosing alveolitis
- upper airway disorders, such as rhinitis and post-nasal drip syndrome

- other bodily system dysfunction such as gastroesophageal reflux disease or heart failure

- medicine usage, particularly angiotensin-converting enzyme (ACE) inhibitors.

Breathlessness (dyspnoea) is defined as a sensation of difficult, laboured or uncomfortable breathing. It might be induced physiologically in response to strenuous exercise and may occasionally have a psychological cause, such as stress. It is essential that every time we see somebody with breathlessness, we consider the following:

Is this breathlessness caused by:

- heart disease?

- lung disease?

- pulmonary vascular disease?

- a systemic disorder (such as anaemia, obesity, or hyperthyroidism)?

- respiratory muscle weakness?

We then need to ask about the speed of onset of the symptoms of breathlessness (acute or gradual?), the circumstances of the breathlessness (for example, on exertion or at rest?; at night or when lying flat?) and ask about associated symptoms and the degree of breathlessness. The ways in which such questioning can enhance diagnostic accuracy are shown in *Table 1*.

With regards to airway disorders, it is important to appreciate that the clinical features of such disorders – cough, wheeze, breathlessness, and obstructive spirometry (an $FEV_1/FVC$ ratio < 0.7) or reduced peak flow – can be common to both *generalised* airway narrowing of medium or small-sized airways or to *localised* obstruction of a larger, more central, airway.

Thus, we need to determine on examination:

- is the wheeze monophonic or polyphonic?

- is the wheeze unilateral?

- is there stridor?

This should enable us to distinguish between localised causes of airway narrowing and generalised causes.

**Table 1.** Breathlessness: differential diagnosis according to speed of onset

| | |
|---|---|
| **Within minutes:** | Think – pulmonary embolus, pneumothorax, myocardial infarction, cardiac rhythm disturbance, dissecting aneurysm, acute asthma. |
| **Over hours or days:** | Think – pneumonia, pleural effusion, LVF (LV dysfunction or valve dysfunction or septal rupture post-myocardial infarction), asthma, blood loss, lobar collapse, respiratory muscle weakness (Guillain Barré). |
| **Over weeks:** | Think – infiltration (malignancy, sarcoidosis, fibrosing alveolitis, extrinsic allergic alveolitis, eosinophilic pneumonia), respiratory muscle weakness (motor neurone disease), main airway obstruction, anaemia, valvular dysfunction (SBE). |
| **Over months:** | Think – same as for weeks, plus obesity, muscular dystrophy, asbestos-related conditions. |
| **Over years:** | Think – COPD, chest wall deformity, heart valve dysfunction, obesity. |

It is then important to realise that, in addition to COPD, the other causes of *generalised* airway narrowing are asthma, bronchiectasis, cystic fibrosis and obliterative bronchiolitis. In the age group in which COPD is possible, the most important differentiation is from asthma, but it is important to exclude suppurative lung disease, such as bronchiectasis. Although asthma and COPD can co-exist, we are often quite sloppy in our differentiation and it is important that we recognise that the causation, the natural history, pathology and management of the two conditions can have significant differences *(see Chapter 2)*. In the future, it is possible that we may have new diagnostic tools to enable a more prompt and accurate differentiation of COPD from asthma. However, at the present time differentiation depends upon being attentive to the clinical features, the use of objective lung function testing, and seeing whether the individual concerned does or does not fulfil the physiological diagnostic definition of asthma, namely:

*"Generalised narrowing of the airways which varies over short periods of time, either spontaneously or as a result of treatment."*

**Table 2.** Differentiation of asthma from COPD

| COPD | Asthma |
|---|---|
| Onset in mid-life<br>Symptoms slowly progressive | Onset usually early in life |
| Smoking history | Symptoms at night or early morning |
| Dyspnoea during exercise | May have associated allergic disease |
| Largely irreversible airflow limitation | Largely reversible airflow limitation |
| | May have family history of asthma |
| | Symptoms vary from day to day |

Both asthma and COPD are relatively common diseases, and it is not surprising, therefore, that the two diseases occasionally occur in the same person. However, the manifestations of the diseases are different and in most cases it is possible to differentiate asthma clearly from COPD. COPD is largely a condition of gradual onset with symptoms that are progressive and come on for the first time in the 5th, 6th or 7th decades of life. This is often quite a different clinical picture to that of asthma, where the symptoms occur both at rest or on exertion, are more likely to be variable, and are usually associated with a personal or family history of allergic disease, often dating back to early life. These features are summarised in *Table 2*.

When evaluating the symptom of breathlessness, we should remember that patients often adapt to slow onset disability. Those in whom a diagnosis of COPD is being considered may unwittingly give misleading responses to questions regarding the onset of symptoms. It is useful to ask when the patient first noted that they were breathless, but to then double-check with subsidiary questions that they had not adapted to the onset of that symptom. This may involve asking questions such as, "Can I just check, then, that you were capable of running the London Marathon 10 years ago?" or, "Can I just check that this time last year, you could have walked home from the supermarket with the

**Table 3.** MRC Dyspnoea grade

1. Normal

2. Able to walk and keep up with people of similar age on the level, but not on hills or stairs.

3. Able to walk for 1.5 km on the level at own pace, but unable to keep up with people of similar age.

4. Able to walk 100 m on the level.

5. Breathless at rest or on minimal effort.

shopping as quickly as I could?" Sometimes it is helpful to record formally the degree of breathlessness and this may be carried out using, for example, the MRC dyspnoea grade *(see Table 3)*.

## Pitfalls in diagnosis and differential diagnosis

A number of other conditions and scenarios may need to be considered and excluded when making a diagnosis of COPD.

### Foreign body inhalation

Foreign body inhalation can occur in the young or the elderly, and it can also occur in those with bulbar disease, the edentulous, and those who are unconscious for any reason, including alcoholics, epileptics and those who have had an accident or operation.

Foreign body inhalation may present with a new-onset cough, breathlessness, stridor or a distal chest infection, and it might present with a normal chest radiograph. Mistakes will be avoided if patients are questioned carefully as to what was happening at the time of onset of the symptoms.

### Diffuse parenchymal lung disease

Diffuse parenchymal lung diseases such as fibrosing alveolitis, asbestosis, or sarcoidosis can present with insidious onset of breathlessness and, in a smoker at least, it is all too easy to attribute such symptoms to COPD. However, patients with the first two conditions at least usually have easily-heard crackles on auscultation; their presence should always lead to spirometric assessment and chest radiography. Sometimes the presence of crackles leads to the incorrect assumption that the patient has heart failure, and anybody with crackles who shows no response to diuretics should similarly be considered possibly to have diffuse parenchymal lung disease.

## Respiratory muscle weakness

Most causes of breathlessness are associated with worsening when the patient is lying flat. We traditionally teach that orthopnoea is a symptom of cardiac failure, but we should always be alert to the possibility of diaphragm weakness as a cause. One semi-acute cause of diaphragm weakness is Guillain Barré syndrome. In patients in their 50s, 60s or 70s presenting with breathlessness that is worse on lying flat, the amyotrophic lateral sclerosis variant of motor neurone disease (which frequently presents in this way) should be considered.

## Pulmonary thromboembolism

The diagnosis of pulmonary embolism is easily missed in elderly patients and those with co-existing cardiorespiratory disease. Although most patients present with pleuritic pain and/or haemoptysis, some present with sudden collapse, and in about a quarter of cases, the presentation is breathlessness without obvious cause. Clues as to the correct diagnosis depend upon ascertaining the presence or absence of risk factors such as immobility, previous DVT or pulmonary embolism, and co-morbidity such as recent surgery, lower limb paralysis, malignancy, chemotherapy, varicose veins, cardiorespiratory disease or infection.

## Lung cancer

Both COPD and lung cancer are related to smoking and both diseases might co-exist. In a smoker or ex-smoker, a new complaint of breathlessness, the presentation of a new cough, or a changed character of a long-standing cough, should always raise a suspicion of lung cancer. Similarly, unexplained weight loss, haemoptysis or depression in a smoker or ex-smoker could suggest the presence of intra-thoracic malignancy.

## Bronchiectasis

While the hyper-secretory component of COPD can be associated with a cough productive of sputum, the quantity of sputum expectorated is usually not great. In any patient presenting with production of sputum of more than a teaspoonful a day, we should be suspicious of an upper airway cause (sinus disease) but, if that is not present, this symptom should lead us to consider bronchiectasis. This is a disease that can easily be missed in primary care, and correct

**Table 4.** Lung diseases

| Infections | |
| --- | --- |
| Tuberculosis | Pneumonia |
| Infective bronchitis | Empyema |

| Pulmonary vascular disorders | |
| --- | --- |
| Pulmonary thromboembolic disease | Primary pulmonary hypertension |
| Pulmonary arteriovenous malformations | |

**Small lung disorders**

These may be due to:

**Lung diseases:**

- Sarcoidosis
- Asbestosis
- Extrinsic allergic alveolitis
- Fibrosing alveolitis
- Eosinophilic pneumonia

**Pleural diseases:**

- Effusions
- Pneumothorax

**Chest wall/muscle disease:**

- Scoliosis
- Respiratory muscle weakness

**Other:**

- Obesity

**Airway diseases**

**Localised:**

- Obstructive sleep apnoea
- Laryngeal carcinoma
- Thyroid enlargement
- Vocal cord dysfunction
- Relapsing polychondritis
- Bronchial and tracheal carcinoma
- Post-tracheostomy stenosis
- Foreign bodies
- Bronchopulmonary dysplasia

**Generalised:**

- Asthma
- COPD
- Bronchiectasis
- Obliterative bronchiolitis

differentiation from COPD is essential because the management is quite different. The definitive diagnosis is often made on CT scan, and so referral should be considered in any patient presenting with frequent episodes of infection or with excess sputum production.

Many of the pitfalls in the diagnosis and differential diagnosis of COPD could be avoided if a logical approach to diagnosis is undertaken. This involves consideration as to whether the symptoms are caused by a disorder of non-pulmonary systems, and then careful differentiation as to whether the symptoms are from a small lung (restrictive) disorder or an airway disorder. The range of these lung disorders is shown in *Table 4*.

This list appears lengthy, but for many diseases the clinical features are characteristic. A chest radiograph is also often helpful in determining whether we are dealing with an infection or small lung disorder or an airway disorder. The use of spirometry in differentiating small lung (restrictive) disorders from obstructive airway disorders is also extremely helpful *(see Chapter 3)*.

In primary care, the golden rule should always apply: if in doubt about the diagnosis, and/or the treatment options seem to be failing, always consider referral for a second opinion. It may well be that making the definitive diagnosis will require CT scanning or more specialised lung function testing.

## Conclusions

A methodical approach to diagnosis, including the history of symptoms, assessment of risk factors and consideration and exclusion of possible alternative diagnoses, should lead to a correct diagnosis of COPD. This can then be backed up by objective assessment using spirometry.

## What could I do?

- At presentation or at re-assessment, always take a good history.

- Remember the variety of conditions, both pulmonary and non-pulmonary, that share symptoms with COPD.

- Distinguish between localised or generalised causes of airways narrowing, and whether the pathology is in large, medium or small airways.

- Consider the diagnostic pitfalls.

## Further reading

The Global Strategy for the Diagnosis, Management, and Prevention of Chronic Obstructive Pulmonary Disease – the GOLD Guidelines, from the National Heart and Lung Institute and the World Health Organisation. NIH publication no. 2701A, March 2001.

National Clinical Guideline on management of chronic obstructive pulmonary disease in adults in primary and secondary care (NICE Guidelines) (2004) *Thorax;* **59** (suppl 1): 1–232.

# Chapter **2**

## The Pathology of COPD

## (chronic bronchitis,

## chronic bronchiolitis and emphysema)

**In this chapter:**

The clinical differences between COPD and asthma are reflected in their respective pathologies.

Descriptions of the inflammation and structural alterations (i.e. remodelling) in COPD and the rationale for pharmacological intervention are given.

COPD and asthma are both obstructive conditions of the lung, each having a major impact in terms of mortality and morbidity respectively. There is a clinical need to distinguish patients in these two categories as they require different approaches to their management and treatment, so that control is maximised and progression of the disease is reduced. Comparison of tissues sampled from the airways of non-smoker asthmatics with reversible disease and smokers with COPD, in which there is 'fixed' airflow obstruction, demonstrates that, while both conditions are associated with chronic inflammation, their pathologies are distinct. It can, however, often be difficult to distinguish COPD from asthma clinically and, depending on smoking history, there might be overlap or both conditions may coexist in the same patient. The diagnosis may be challenging especially in the older asthmatic who develops a degree of irreversible airflow obstruction. Interestingly, it has recently been shown that, in spite of this clinical overlap, examination of the airway tissues can still discriminate these two conditions Before considering the distinctive nature of the inflammation and of the alterations of airway and parenchymal tissue structure in COPD (the structural changes usually grouped under the heading of remodelling), we begin with a brief resume of what we know about asthma.

## Asthma

In fatal asthma, the airways post mortem are found to be occluded by highly tenacious plugs of exudate mixed with mucus. There is fragility and variable loss of the airway surface ciliated epithelium that normally lines the conducting airways. There is a characteristic thickening of the reticular basement membrane (RBM) that normally provides support to the overlying epithelium. Detection of this aspect of remodelling, together with an eosinophil-rich infiltrate of inflammatory cells, is compatible with the diagnosis of asthma. Further immunohistological characterisation of the inflammatory cells that infiltrate the airway wall in asthma also demonstrates the presence of mast cells and 'activated' T-lymphocytes (T-cells), predominantly of the CD4+ or 'T-helper' phenotype, a pattern of inflammation characteristic of an allergic response. In mild to moderate asthma, T-helper cells outnumber CD8+ T-cytotoxic/suppressor cells by about 3:1. Eosinophils, T-helper cells and mast cells are usually reduced relatively rapidly in response to treatment with inhaled corticosteroids, at least in the larger airways that are accessible to investigation by the technique of flexible fibre-optic bronchoscopy (FOB) and endobronchial biopsy. In mild asthma, there are few tissue neutrophils ('polymorphs') but numbers may increase markedly in severe (corticosteroid-resistant) asthma and when there are acute exacerbations of asthma. Other important structural changes in the asthmatic airway wall include: proliferation and congestion of bronchial vessels (the systemic blood supply to the airways); and oedema and enlargement of the mass of bronchial smooth muscle, which constricts the airways. The last aspect of remodelling is particularly obvious in large, proximal bronchi of patients who have died of their asthma. By FOB investigation, most of these changes are found to be present already in young adults with newly diagnosed asthma and they are even present in the bronchial wall of children (between the ages of 5 and 15 years) with asthma that has been difficult to manage.

## COPD

Like asthma, COPD is also an inflammatory condition but, in contrast, the pattern of inflammation is distinct and all airway generations and the lung parenchyma are affected. There is chronic inflammation of large central bronchi – the airways *(Fig. 1)* with supportive cartilage in their walls – (i.e. chronic bronchitis), and inflammation of small membranous bronchioli, airways that lack cartilage (i.e. chronic bronchiolitis). There is loss of the alveolar walls in the lung parenchyma with resultant destructive enlargement of airspaces beyond the

**Figure 1.** CD8+ inflammatory cells in COPD

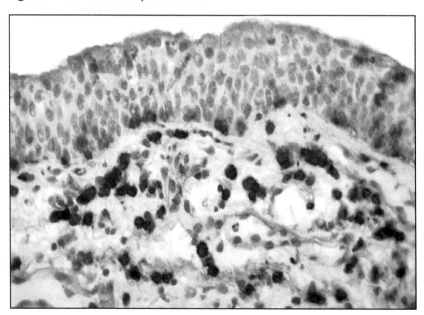

terminal bronchioli (i.e. emphysema). The inflammation and remodelling of the large airways are the alterations that are most responsible for the hypersecretion of mucus, the excess that is chronically expectorated by cough (as sputum) and the basis for the clinical definition of chronic bronchitis. Alterations in bronchioles of < 2 mm diameter and lung parenchyma are considered to be those changes most responsible for the lung function deficit and accelerated decline of $FEV_1$ characteristic of COPD. In addition there is inflammation and remodelling of pulmonary arteries, that closely accompany the airways, and also systemic inflammation and structural alterations of skeletal muscle that contribute significantly to symptoms, progression, disability and mortality. These anatomic compartments are now considered each in turn.

## Chronic bronchitis or 'mucus-hypersecretion'

### Excess mucus

Normally, cilia and mucus work together to clear mucus, with adsorbed pollutant gases and particles, viruses and bacteria to the throat where they are imperceptivity swallowed. When there is failure of the mucociliary system,

**Figure 2.** Mucus-hypersecretion in chronic bronchitis

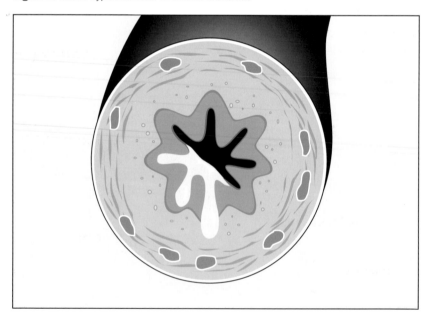

cough is required to clear increased lumenal secretions *(Fig. 2)*. This is effective only to about the 6th generation of airway branching. The majority of the increased mucus expectorated as sputum is the result of a combination of increased size (i.e. hypertrophy) and inflammation of tracheo-bronchial glands situated deep in the tracheo-bronchial wall. The types of inflammatory cell infiltrating the glands include mast cells, neutrophils and lymphocytes. The presence of large numbers of plasma cells has also recently been reported. Each of these cell types is able to secrete distinct chemicals that induce the rapid discharge of mucus from the glands. There is also an increase in the numbers of pre-existing epithelial goblet cells, a process referred to as goblet cell hyperplasia, and this forms an additional source for the increased mucus. The remodelling and hypertrophy of mucous glands can also occur in asthma. In contrast to asthma, the RBM beneath the epithelium is *not* normally thickened in COPD. There are, however, some patients with COPD that have (as expected) poor airway reversibility to β-agonists, who may, however, demonstrate a relatively substantial degree of airways reversibility to a (14-day) course of *oral* cortico-steroids. Interestingly these patients have a significantly thicker epithelial RBM [and an increased bronchoalveolar lavage (BAL) eosinophilia] than the COPD patients who do not show such reversibility, and thus this example provides evidence for the overlap (in both remodelling and inflammation) that can exist between COPD and asthma *(Fig. 3)*.

**Figure 3.** Chronic inflammatory lung disease: inter-relationships

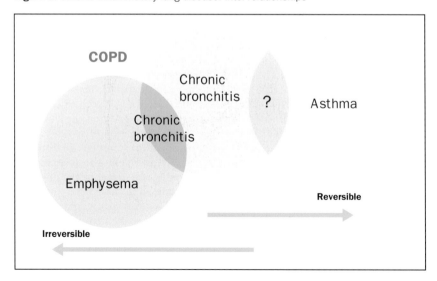

## Inflammation

There is an approximately threefold increase above the normal in the overall numbers of immune cells in the airway mucosa in COPD and T-lymphocytes are again frequent, as in asthma. However, in contrast to the non-smokers with asthma, smokers with COPD have relatively greater numbers of CD8+ cells than CD4+ cells, i.e. the ratio of T-helper to T-cytotoxic cells found in normal healthy individuals and asthmatics is reversed in COPD, there now being a predominance of the T-cytotoxic subset of T-cells *(Fig 1)*. In the international guideline for COPD, the 'GOLD' guidelines, this pattern of inflammation has been referred to as 'abnormal'. Also, in contrast to asthma, tissue eosinophils are rarely found in mild stable COPD and instead there are increased numbers of macrophages. Apart from the mast cells, which are often also increased in number, this pattern of inflammation is less likely to be reduced by corticosteroid therapy. Importantly, the pattern of inflammation found in mild stable COPD changes markedly in association with an exacerbation (when there is acute worsening of symptoms, an increase in sputum volume, purulence and increased dyspnoea). In exacerbations of COPD, a tissue neutrophilia and eosinophilia develops. In contrast to the pattern of inflammation of stable COPD, the eosinophilia and inflammatory mediators responsible for the recruitment of eosinophils in exacerbations of COPD are likely to be attenuated by corticosteroid therapy, as there are several previous reports to show that eosinophils (and mast cells) can be reduced in number following such treatment.

## Chronic bronchiolitis or 'small (peripheral) airways disease'

The progressive decline of lung function (i.e. $FEV_1$) characteristic of COPD is associated more with alterations occurring in small airways of < 2 mm diameter (i.e. beyond the 8th airway division) than those related to mucus-hypersecretion in the large airways (i.e. the first eight divisions of branching). These intrapulmonary airways are relatively thin-walled and lack the supportive cartilage plates that define bronchi. Instead, for their patency, they rely on the elasticity of the many alveolar walls that attach to the outer circumference (adventitia) of their walls and link them (eventually) to the pleura of the lung *(Fig. 4)*. Thus, as the chest wall expands the alveoli stretch radially and help also to open the conducting airway. Even more critical, the stored elastic recoil in the alveolar walls maintains the airway open during expiration as intra-alveolar pressure rises. Damage or loss of these alveolar-bronchiolar attachments would result in collapse and blockage of these otherwise unsupported small airways.

**Figure 4.** Small airway: normal bronchiole and surrounding alveoli

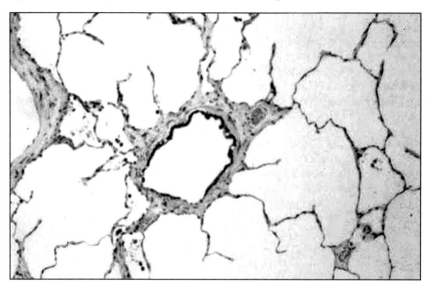

**Figure 5.** Small airway: inflammation: COPD

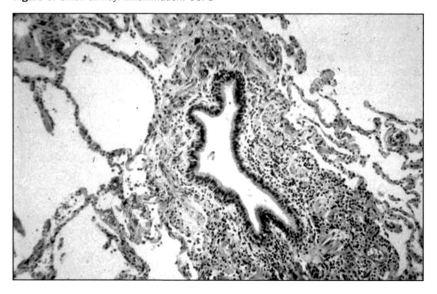

## Mucus

Normally, mucus is absent from bronchioli, because of the absence at this site of mucus-secreting glands and epithelial goblet cells. However, in COPD, goblet cells appear in the epithelium and increase in number to produce mucus. This process of transformation of a non mucus-producing epithelium to one that secretes it is called "mucous or goblet cell metaplasia". The resultant accumulation of mucus at this peripheral anatomic site is extremely difficult to clear by cough and contributes further to blockage of small airways and reduction of the ratio of $FEV_1$/forced vital capacity (FVC).

## Inflammation

The predominant pattern of inflammatory cell infiltration is again cytotoxic T-cells. There is also a respiratory bronchiolitis in which there are increased numbers of pigmented (smoke-laden) macrophages, considered to be a critically important early lesion in cigarette smokers. Increasingly severe peribronchiolitis contributes to both a thickening of the bronchiolar wall and loss of the alveolar attachments, allowing the small airways to shut-off during expiration at an earlier stage than is normal (Fig. 5). Increasing mucus and inflammation in these small airways and loss of alveolar attachments are associated with air trapping, hyperinflation and breathing at higher than normal lung volumes. These changes may predispose to the development of emphysema.

## Other structural changes

Increased wall muscle occurs in the small (not large) airways and is associated with reduced $FEV_1$. There is also an increase in the laying down of collagen (i.e. fibrosis), and focal airway stenoses. There are also reports that inflammation of small airways may occur when asthma is severe and associated with nocturnal symptoms and reduced lung function.

# Emphysema

Emphysema is defined as abnormal, permanent enlargement of airspaces distal to the terminal bronchiolus, accompanied by destruction of alveolar walls, without obvious fibrosis (there are, however, some reports of focal fibrosis). The emphysema that occurs in cigarette smokers is referred to as centri-lobular (or centri-acinar) emphysema as it is centred in areas around the conducting airways. It is also most characteristically found and worst in the upper aspects of each lung lobe (Fig. 6).

Although COPD can be diagnosed in the absence of obvious emphysema (when small airway changes may be the major driver of reduced lung function), the

**Figure 6.** Centri-lobular emphysema *(by courtesy of Prof B. Heard)*

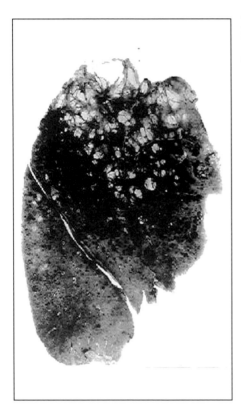

presence and severity of emphysema is an important determinant of chronic deterioration of airflow. There can also be significant loss of lung elastic recoil due to microscopic emphysema prior to the observed macroscopic destruction of lung parenchyma (i.e. when airspaces are > 1mm and may be ≥ 1cm (the last termed 'bullae').

## Inflammation

Once again, it is the increased presence of T-lymphocytes that are associated with loss of parenchymal tissue and the increase in the number of T-cytotoxic cells in the alveolar walls that correlate with the reduced values for $FEV_1$ in COPD. In severe emphysema there is also a correlation between the numbers of macrophages in the alveolar air spaces and increasing severity of emphysema. In contrast emphysema is not a feature of asthma, at least in individuals who do not smoke.

## Hypotheses

There are several hypotheses to explain the destruction of lung tissue in emphysema:

- an imbalance due to a disproportionate increase of proteases (from inflammatory cells and other sources), which overwhelms antiproteases (normally present) thus favouring proteolytic destruction of lung tissue

- an imbalance of oxidants and antioxidants favouring oxidant-mediated damage

- loss, particularly of capillary endothelial cells, due to a process of programmed cell death (apoptosis).

Although the loss of lung parenchyma in humans is considered to be irreversible there are intriguing results in experimental animals suggesting that new alveolar walls and alveoli have the potential to be re-formed. Whether or not this is also possible in humans has yet to be determined.

## Other changes in COPD

### Pulmonary arteries

There is thickening of the pulmonary vascular walls early in the development of COPD. Intimal thickening (i.e. of the inner lining of vessels) is an early change associated with smoking and inflammation of the arterial wall. In addition, an increase of vascular smooth muscle in the media of small muscular arteries is a response associated with the chronic hypoxia that develops following the widespread blockage of small airways that leads to reflex arterial constriction (normally a protective response designed to shunt blood to better-ventilated areas of the lung in order to match perfusion to ventilation). Associated with this is a rise in intravascular pulmonary pressure that imparts strain on the right heart and initiates the development of right ventricular hypertrophy (secondary to the lung disease; i.e. *cor pulmonale*). Recent studies have demonstrated that there is also infiltration of the pulmonary artery adventitia by inflammatory cells, particularly T-cytotoxic cells, and that this increase is also associated with reduced $FEV_1$. There is even a relative increase in T-cytotoxic cells seen in the lymphatic system that drains the lung.

### Systemic effects

In heavy smokers, even without COPD there is a relative increase in T-cytotoxic cells in the circulation. Additional extrapulmonary or systemic effects include an increase in blood borne circulating inflammatory mediators (e.g. TNF α), acute phase protein-associated molecules (e.g. IL6, fibrinogen and C-reactive protein) and wasting of skeletal muscle (resulting from muscle cell death). These systemic effects are reflected in patient weight loss (reduced body mass index; BMI), loss of muscle mass and dysfunction and impaired exercise tolerance.

## Conclusions

The individual's genetic background, smoking habit and viral infection can each have a major influence on the high T-cytotoxic/T-helper ratio characteristic of smokers with COPD. Finally, whereas corticosteroids do not appear to affect the numbers of T-cytotoxic cells in the airway tissue of smokers with COPD, the numbers of mast cells can be reduced with inhaled corticosteroids over a

3-month period, and there are recently described new compounds (e.g. the selective phosphodiesterase-4 inhibitors) that reduce the numbers of T-cytotoxic cells and macrophages in COPD. However, the relationship between these effects of selected anti-inflammatory therapy, the predominant pattern of inflammation in COPD and the progressive and accelerated decline of lung function in COPD has yet to be determined.

## What could I do?

■ An appreciation of the pathology of COPD, its pathological distinction from asthma and how the patterns of inflammation change in association with exacerbations helps with diagnosis, education and decisions about clinical management.

## Further reading

Chanez, P., Vignola, A.M., O'Shaughnessy, T., Enander, I., Li, D., Jeffery, P.K., et al. (1997) Corticosteroid reversibility in COPD is related to features of asthma. Am. J. Respir. Crit. Care Med., **155**:1529–1534.

Gamble, E., Grootendorst, D.C., Brightling, C.E., Troy, S., Qiu, Y., Zhu, J., et al (2003) Antiinflammatory effects of the phosphodiesterase-4 inhibitor cilomilast (ariflo) in chronic obstructive pulmonary disease. Am. J. Respir. Crit. Care Med., **168**:976–982.

Hamid, Q., Song, Y., Kotsimbos, T.C., Minshall, E., Bai, T.R., Hegele, R.G., et al. (1997) Inflammation of small airways in asthma. J. Allergy Clin. Immunol., **100**:44–51.

Hattotuwa, K.L., Gizycki, M.J., Ansari, T.W., Jeffery, P.K. and Barnes, N.C. (2002) The effects of inhaled fluticasone on airway inflammation in chronic obstructive pulmonary disease: a double-blind, placebo-controlled biopsy study. Am. J. Respir.Crit. Care Med., **165**:1592–1596.

Jeffery, P.K. (2001) Lymphocytes, chronic bronchitis and chronic obstructive pulmonary disease. In Chadwick, D. & Goode, J.A. (eds) Chronic Obstructive Pulmonary Disease: Pathogenesis to Treatment. John Wiley & Sons Ltd, Chichester, pp. 149–168.

Jeffery, P.K. (2001) Remodeling in asthma and chronic obstructive lung disease. Am. J. Respir. Crit. Care Med., **164**:S28–S38.

Jeffery, P.K. and Saetta, M. (2003) Pathology of chronic obstructive pulmonary disease. In Gibson, G.J., Geddes, D.M., Costabel, U., Sterk, P.J. and Corrin, B. (eds) Respiratory Medicine, Third edition. Saunders, London, pp. 1141–1153.

Lams, B.E., Sousa, A.R., Rees, P.J. and Lee, T.H. (1998) Immunopathology of the small-airway submucosa in smokers with and without chronic obstructive pulmonary disease. *Am. J. Respir. Crit. Care Med.*, **158**:1518–1523.

Lams, B.E., Sousa, A.R., Rees, P.J. and Lee, T.H. (2000) Subepithelial immunopathology of large airways in smokers with and without chronic obstructive pulmonary disease. *Eur. Respir. J.*, **15**:512–516.

O'Shaughnessy, T., Ansari, T.W., Barnes, N.C. and Jeffery, P.K. (1997) Inflammation in bronchial biopsies of subjects with chronic bronchitis: inverse relationship of CD8+ T lymphocytes with FEV1. *Am. J. Respir. Crit. Care Med.*, **155**:852–857.

Qiu, Y., Zhu, J., Bandi, V., Atmar, L., Hattotuwa, K., Guntupalli, K.K., *et al.* (2003) Biopsy neutrophilia, neutrophil chemokine and receptor gene expression in severe exacerbations of chronic obstructive pulmonary disease. *Am. J.Respir.Crit. Care Med.*, **168**:968–975.

Retamales, I., Elliott, W.M., Meshi, B., Coxson, H.O., Pare, P.D., Sciurba, F.C., *et al.* (2001) Amplification of inflammation in emphysema and its association with latent adenoviral infection. *Am. J. Respir. Crit. Care Med.*, **164**:469–473.

Saetta, M., Baraldo, S., Corbino, L., Turato, G., Braccioni, F., Rea, F., *et al.* (1999) CD8+ cells in the lungs of smokers with chronic obstructive pulmonary disease. *Am. J. Respir. Crit. Care Med.*, **160**:711–717.

Saetta, M., Di Stefano, A., Maestrelli, P., Turato, G., Ruggieri, P., Calcagni, P., *et al.* (1994) Airway eosinophilia in chronic bronchitis during exacerbations. *Am. J. Respir. Crit. Care Med.*, **150**:1646–1652.

Saetta, M., Di Stefano, A., Turato, G., Facchini, F., Corbino, L., Mapp, C.E., *et al.* (1998) CD8+ T-lymphocytes in peripheral airways of smokers with chronic obstructive pulmonary disease. *Am. J. Respir. Crit. Care Med.*, **157**:822–826.

Wang, J.H., Devalia, J.L., Sapsford, R.J. and Davies, R.J. (1997) Effect of corticosteroids on release of RANTES and sICAM-1 from cultured human bronchial epithelial cells, induced by TNF-alpha. *Eur. Respir. J.*, **10**:834–840.

Zhu, J., Qiu, Y.S., Majumdar, S., Gamble, E., Matin, D., Turato, G., *et al.* (2001) Bronchial eosinophilia and gene expression for IL-4, IL-5, and eosinophil chemoattractants in bronchitis. *Am. J. Respir. Crit. Care Med.*, **164**:109–116.

Zhu, J., Majumdar, S., Qiu, Y.S., Ansari, T., Oliva, A., Kips, J.C., *et al.* (2001) IL-4 and IL-5 gene expression and inflammation in the mucus-secreting glands and subepithelial tissue of smokers with chronic bronchitis: lack of relationship with CD8+ cells. *Am. J. Respir. Crit. Care Med.*, **164**:2220–2228.

# Chapter **3**

## Spirometry: an Introduction

**In this chapter:**

The diagnosis of COPD cannot be confirmed without performing spirometry.

The principles of spirometry and its interpretation are detailed

The different volume/time curves for obstructive and restrictive lung disease are discussed.

Definitions of FEV1 and FVC, the principles of % predicted values and the FEV1/FVC ratio are given.

Spirometry is a simple method for studying lung function. A spirometer records the volume movement of air into and out of the lungs over time. Although modern spirometers can quantify a large variety of different measurements of lung function, in primary care only the expiratory function is routinely performed, and in particular, only two measurements are commonly obtained and analysed – forced expiratory volume in the first second ($FEV_1$) and forced vital capacity (FVC). Some years ago, with the advent of simple and easily available peak expiratory flow meters, and a focus on the management of asthma at the expense of COPD, the routine use of spirometry fell into decline somewhat. Although measurement of peak flow can be very useful in the diagnosis and assessment of asthma, it has almost no value in the management of COPD. The prominence given to spirometry in national and international COPD guidelines, and the introduction of the new general practice GMS contract, has led to a renewed interest in spirometric techniques and interpretation – by definition, an accurate diagnosis of COPD requires the objective demonstration of airflow obstruction.

## The physiology of the lung

*Figure 7* illustrates the physiological lung volume components during different breathing (or ventilation) conditions. The **tidal volume** is the volume of air inspired or expired with each normal breath, usually about 500 ml; the **inspiratory reserve volume** is the amount of air that can be inspired over and above normal tidal volume, and in a healthy adult is usually about 3l; and the **expiratory reserve volume** is the amount of air that can be expelled forcibly after normal tidal volume expiration (usually about 1l). These three volumes add up to the **vital capacity**, the maximum amount of air that a person can expel from the lungs after first filling their lungs to the maximum volume.

Predicted values for these volumes depend upon the person's age, gender and height. In a young man, for example, the vital capacity will be about 4.5l. In women, the pulmonary volumes are approximately 20% less than in men, and over the age of 30 the pulmonary volumes gradually decrease with increasing age. In addition, a tall person will have higher pulmonary volumes (for a given age and gender) than a shorter person.

## Simple spirometry

The two simplest (and most useful) measurements obtained by spirometry are the FVC and the $FEV_1$. The FVC is the amount of air that one can blow out forcefully after a maximal inspiration *(see Fig. 8)*. In a normal person the vast majority

**Figure 7.** A basic spirometry tracing showing lung volume against time during different breathing conditions

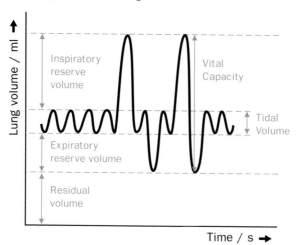

of that air is blown out within the first second, so that when the $FEV_1$ is expressed as a percentage of the FVC, the percentage is roughly 75%. (In fact this figure varies a little with age in normal subjects, such that a fit young person would expect to blow out 80% of their vital capacity in the first second, whereas a very elderly person may only blow out 65–67%). This percentage (or $FEV_1$/FVC ratio) is a crucial part of interpreting spirometry. In those with airway narrowing, whether from asthma or COPD, the key feature is that it takes the person longer to blow out the air from their airways. Their FVC may indeed be reduced (because of gas trapping beyond closed airways, or in the case of COPD because of alveolar distortion and destruction) but they only manage to blow out, say, 30– 60% of their vital capacity in the first second. In contrast , in those with a small lung (volume) disorder (often unhelpfully referred to as a restrictive defect), the vital capacity is reduced but there is nothing wrong with the airways, so the patient still blows out 75–80% of their FVC in the first second. When interpreting spirometric tracings, the sequence should therefore be as follows:

Is the FVC normal for that person's age, gender and height, and, if so, did they blow out more than 70% of that vital capacity in the first second? If they did, the result is normal. If they blew out less than 70%, they have an obstructive defect, i.e. airways narrowing (commonly COPD or asthma).

If, on the other hand, the FVC is reduced, we then look at how much they were able to blow out in the first second and if it is less than 70% the patient again has evidence of airway narrowing; if it is more than 70%, the patient has a small lung disorder.

With regards to small lung disorders it is very important to remember that this may occur because of a problem with the lungs themselves (such as fibrosing alveolitis, sarcoidosis, infection or infiltration); or the lungs may be small because of a problem outside the lungs (such as a large pleural effusion or a chest wall deformity such as kyphoscoliosis); or the lungs may be small because of an inability to take a deep breath because of, for example, diaphragmatic weakness; or finally the lungs may be small because of the constricting corset-like effect of obesity.

Predicted normal values for $FEV_1$ and FVC are available from a number of sources. The values currently used in the UK are those of the European Community for Steel and Coal. These may lead to under-diagnosis in the elderly and need adjustment in black and Asian populations.

## Spirometry tracing and interpretation

The $FEV_1$ and FVC readings obtained can be compared with these predicted values, and we can therefore express $FEV_1$ and FVC as absolute values in litres

**Figure 8.** Spirometry tracing obtained following a forced expiratory manoeuvre, from a patient with normal airways showing FEV1 and FVC values and normal FEV1/FVC ratio

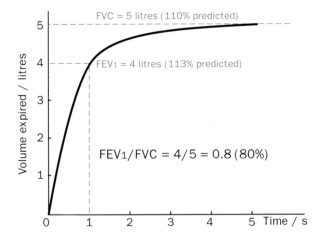

but also in terms of their **percent (%) predicted** value. Thus, using the example in *Fig. 8*, the $FEV_1$ is 4 l and the FVC is 5 l. Let us assume that the $FEV_1$ is 113% predicted and the FVC is 110% predicted for this patient's age, gender and height. Our patient in *Fig. 8* has produced a normal value for FVC, and the $FEV_1/FVC$ percentage (or ratio) is 4/5, 80% or 0.8. This is, therefore, a normal tracing.

**Figure 9a.** Spirometry tracing of a patient with COPD – an *obstructive* picture

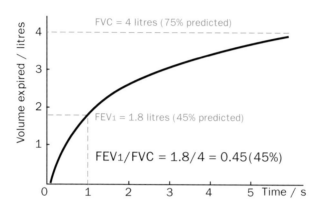

**Figure 9b.** Spirometry tracing of a patient with fibrosing alveolitis – a *restrictive* (small lung) picture

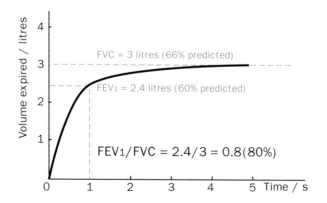

The accepted definition of obstructive airways disease is that the $FEV_1/FVC$ ratio is < 0.7 (percentage < 70%). *Fig. 9a* shows the volume/time spirometry tracing for a patient with COPD. The FVC in this case is 4 l (let us assume that this is 75% predicted) and the $FEV_1$ is 1.8 l (let us assume 45% predicted). The $FEV_1/FVC$ ratio is, therefore:

$$\frac{1.8}{4.0} = 0.45$$

This is less than 0.7, and confirms the obstructive picture.

*Fig. 9b* shows a different sort of tracing. This patient has an $FEV_1$ of 2.4 l (assume 60% predicted) and an FVC of 3 l (say, 66% predicted). The $FEV_1/FVC$ ratio is:

$$\frac{2.4}{3.0} = 0.8$$

so this is a normal ratio, and certainly not an obstructive picture. The curve looks similar to that shown in *Fig. 8*. The tracing is abnormal though, because the volumes are less than expected. This is, therefore, most likely to be a small lung disease (a '**restrictive** picture'), and one needs to consider all of the differential diagnoses given earlier.

Another way of expressing these volume/time curves (the normal curve is reproduced again in *Fig. 10a*) is to plot flow (the rate at which air is being expelled) against the volume of air that has been expelled from the lungs at that point. This produces a **flow/volume curve**, and as the data relates solely to the patient's forced expiratory manoeuvre, this is therefore the **expiratory** flow/volume curve *(see Fig. 10b)*. In *Fig. 10a*, the greatest flow is at the start of forced expiration, the point at which the gradient of the curve is steepest. Therefore, the highest flow rate (the vertical axis) in *10b* is just after the beginning of the curve, when there is most of the volume of air still to be expelled – a flow rate of over 5 l/s. The horizontal axis in *Fig. 10b* shows the volume expired, starting from zero, and finishing with 5 l – equivalent to the FVC as shown in *Fig. 10a*. Thus, the flow/volume curve shows a very rapid increase in flow at the start of expiration, reaches its peak quickly, and then there is an increasingly rapid reduction in flow rate as the forced expiration finishes, with the curve dropping to zero flow rate at a point corresponding to the FVC, i.e. 5 l. The peak

**Figure 10a.** A normal volume/time curve (spirogram)

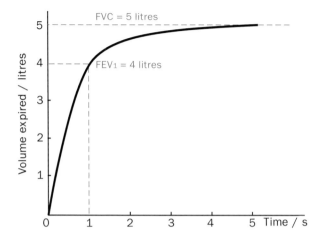

**Figure 10b.** A flow/volume curve using the same data obtained at the same time from the same forced expiratory manoeuvre, but plotted differently

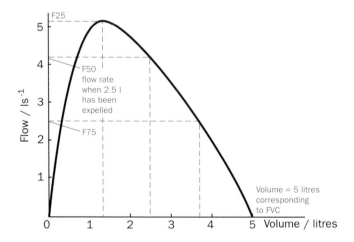

**Figure 11.** Normal flow/volume curve compared with that from an asthma patient showing volume-dependent airway collapse, reduced F50 value and 'concave' shape of the flow/volume curve after 2 litres has been expelled

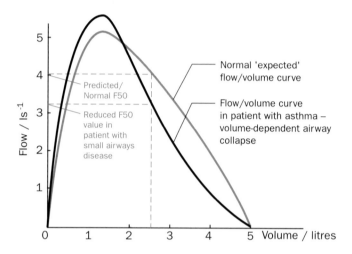

of the expiratory flow/volume curve is, of course, the **peak expiratory flow**, in this case 5 l/s, equivalent to 300 l/min.

The shape of the flow/volume curve can be expressed quantitatively in terms of the flow rate occurring at various volume points – in particular the flow rate corresponding to the point at which 50% of the volume has been expired; this is the **F50 value**. In *Fig. 10b*, the F50 is the flow rate occurring when 2.5 litres has been expired (about 4.3 l/s). One can also obtain **F25 and F75 values** – the flow rates when 25% and 75% of the FVC volume have been expired – in this case 5.25 and 2.5 l/s, respectively.

There are three major patterns of flow–volume curve. The normal curve follows almost a straight line from the peak flow point at the top of the curve down to the x-axis – the volume corresponding to the FVC value. If, however, there is a 'concave' or 'scalloped' shape to the expiratory flow–volume curve (as shown in *Fig. 11*) this signifies volume-dependent airway collapse, a picture seen in asthma or COPD when there is still considerable elasticity of the airways.

Finally, an expiratory flow-volume curve which shows pressure-dependent airway collapse, as shown in *Fig. 12b*, is very suggestive of emphysema, showing profound loss of lung elasticity. There will be a severely reduced flow rate, particularly after the first second or so of forced expiration, and this gives the

**Figure 12a.** The Volume/time curve for a patient with severe COPD

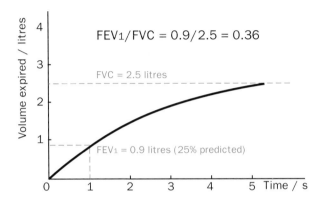

**Figure 12b.** The corresponding flow/volume curve for a patient with severe COPD. Note the 'church steeple' shape of the curve

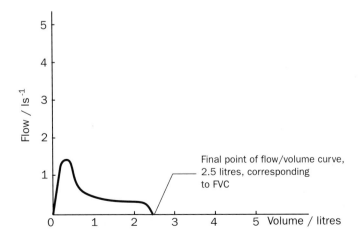

**Figure 13.** The flow/volume loop obtained from a patient with normal airways and an FVC of 5 litres

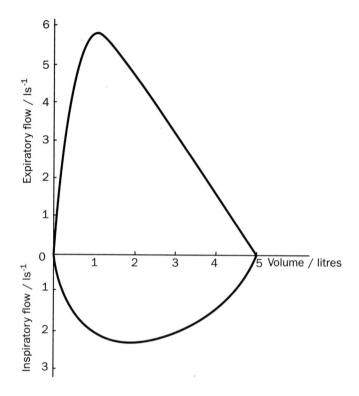

curve the characteristic appearance of a 'church steeple' The maximum flow rate obtained is considerably less than normal, and the overall volume expired is, of course, reduced as per the reduced FVC.

In a General Practice surgery or outpatient clinic, the above data are obtained relatively easily from the forced expiratory manoeuvre, and there are guidelines from both UK and international bodies regarding the techniques that need to be employed, including calibration of the spirometer, in order to obtain consistent and reproducible recordings. However, specialised lung function laboratories have more sophisticated equipment that can assess **inspiration** as well as expiration, and a **flow/volume loop** can be obtained *(as shown in Fig. 13).*

## Conclusions

We are now in a position to be able to interpret most of the spirometry tracings that can be obtained in primary care.

Spirometry is essential in the management of COPD both for confirming the diagnosis, but also for assessing its severity and its progression over time. However, it is also an essential and easy-to-use tool in a wide variety of respiratory illnesses, not just COPD, and is also invaluable for differentiating the causes of breathlessness (which may result from lung disease, heart disease, muscle weakness or system disorders such as anaemia or obesity).

---

### What could I do?

■ Ensure that your practice has access to spirometry.

■ Undertake, or request, spirometry in all patients with suspected COPD at the time of diagnosis and at intervals thereafter
*(see Chapter 1).*

■ If spirometry is undertaken in the Practice, confirm adequate training for all clinicians involved in procedure and interpretation.

■ Ensure that the spirometer is serviced and calibrated regularly.

---

## Further reading

Gibson G.J., Respiratory Function Tests. In: Warrell D.A., Weatherall D.J., Cox T.M., Benz E.J., Firth J.D., eds. *Oxford Textbook of Medicine.* 4th edn. Oxford: OUP; 1304-1307

# Chapter 4

## COPD as a Systemic Disease

**In this chapter:**

Although the primary pathology in COPD is in the airways and lung parenchyma, it is now acknowledged that the inflammatory process that results in the abnormalities in the respiratory system also cause systemic effects.

The most important and well studied of these systemic effects are nutritional depletion and muscle wasting.

In patients with COPD, irrespective of the severity of the disease, a low BMI and weight loss are associated with increased mortality and morbidity; patients with a low BMI have a decreased exercise capacity and suffer more frequent exacerbations.

All patients with COPD should have their height and weight measured at baseline and BMI computed; seeking a history of weight loss and measurement of body weight should be an integral part of the review of patients with moderate to severe COPD.

Lung cancer must be considered as a cause of weight loss in these patients; a chest X-ray is mandatory in COPD patients losing weight.

COPD patients with an abnormal BMI (< 20 and > 28) may benefit from a referral for specialist advice.

Weight gain in malnourished COPD patients is associated with an improved prognosis; however, prescription of nutritional supplements *ad libitum* without adequate specialist supervision is not recommended.

Some studies have shown an increased prevalence of depression and anxiety in patients with COPD, particularly those who have severe disease, are hypoxic and are hospitalised frequently for the condition.

Depression and anxiety states must be actively sought in these patient groups and managed appropriately; pharmacotherapy for depression without adequate explanation is associated with poor concordance with such treatment.

Although the main tissue damage that results from the uncontrolled inflammatory cascade initiated by cigarette smoking is in the airways and lung parenchyma, there is much evidence to suggest that these inflammatory mechanisms extend beyond the chest to cause systemic effects. The most important of these systemic effects are nutritional depletion and weight loss, which occur in as many as a third of COPD patients with moderate to severe disease. Not uncommonly, there are also mental health problems, such as depression and anxiety, associated with the disease. Although the exact pathophysiology of these systemic effects, the reasons why they affect some, but not all, COPD patients, and how they vary in relation to the severity of airflow obstruction and hypoxia remain to determined, the undeniable negative impact of these effects on the overall prognosis of COPD is enough to warrant due attention and appropriate management. This chapter describes the effects of COPD on the nutritional and mental health status of patients with the disease and provides some practical advice on the management of these conditions in the context of COPD.

## Nutrition in COPD

The classification of COPD patients into extremes of body types: the cachectic 'pink puffer' (breathless and tachypnoeic at rest; 'can't breathe'; *see Fig. 14*); and the corpulent 'blue bloater' (cyanosed and hypoventilating at rest; 'won't breathe'; *see Fig. 15*) has helped to focus attention on the nutritional consequences of COPD. We now know, however, that such a division of COPD patients into two distinct categories is rather artificial and in many ways misleading. However, the underlying principle that COPD has a significant effect on the nutritional status and body form of many patients is now acknowledged. The main reason for the renewed interest in the area is the recognition that weight loss and nutritional depletion, irrespective of the severity of airflow obstruction, is associated with a greater mortality and morbidity. Even when patients with moderately severe disease lose significant body weight, they suffer a greater mortality and morbidity (suffer more frequent exacerbations and hospitalisations; have poorer exercise capacity and quality of life) than their weight-stable peers.

## Prevalence and scale of the problem

Low body weight is the most easily measured sign of poor nutritional status. The body mass index (BMI) is a useful method of standardising body weight for height and is calculated by dividing body weight (expressed in kg) by the square of height (in metres). A BMI of 20–25 is the normal range. Studies using a BMI of < 20 or a weight loss of 5% in the preceding 6 months as indicators of

**Figure 14.** 'Pink puffer'          **Figure 15.** 'Blue bloater'

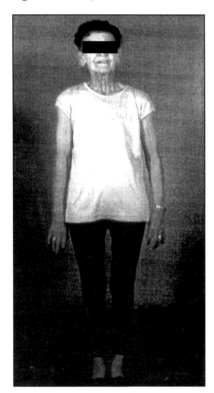 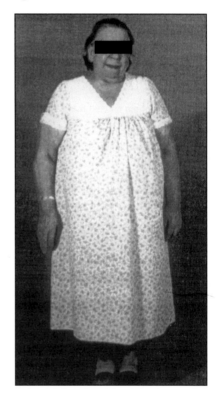

a poor and deteriorating nutritional status indicate a 10–20% prevalence of these states in patients with moderate to severe COPD. More sophisticated measures that identify loss of lean body mass (i.e. non-fat or mainly muscle mass) by special techniques like bio-impedence or dual X-ray absorptiometry show that a further number (around 5–10%) of COPD patients will have a normal body weight but a decreased lean body mass. Therefore, overall between one-fifth and one-third of COPD patients with moderate to severe disease might suffer from a depleted nutritional status. However, other studies have also identified that approximately 10% of COPD patients are overweight (studies mostly define being overweight as a BMI of > 28 and being obese as a BMI of > 30). Thus a significant proportion of COPD patients suffer from a state of altered nutrition – either under- or over-nutrition – which has an adverse impact on their prognosis.

**Table 5.** Factors that might contribute to weight loss in COPD

---

Increased energy expenditure due to increased work of breathing

Energy cost of recurrent infections

Poor oral intake caused by: (a) breathlessness related to eating; and, (b) depression

Hypoxia related to deranged gas exchange

Metabolic effect of therapy (β-agonists, theophyllines); steroids (although causing weight gain, steroids deplete muscle mass)

---

## Mechanisms of weight loss in COPD

The exact mechanisms that lead to weight loss in COPD, and why only some patients, but not others, lose weight is unclear. There are a number of factors that have been identified as causing a state of negative energy balance and thus lead to weight loss in the condition *(Table 5)*. It is, however, clear that impairment of gas exchange (as measured by a decreased diffusing capacity) is a better predictor of weight loss and malnutrition than measures of airflow obstruction ($FEV_1$) *per se*. In COPD patients who are losing weight, it would appear that there is enhanced activity of various cytokines, such as tumour necrosis factor-α (TNF-α) and interleukin-6 (IL-6), that usually mediate cachexia, but exactly how and why these cytokines are activated is not known.

## Management of nutritional problems in COPD

Reliable identification is the first step towards appropriate management of nutritional problems associated with COPD. All COPD patients should undergo measurement of their body weight, height and computation of their BMI at baseline, and all patients with moderate to severe disease should be asked for the history of their weight loss. A BMI of < 20 or > 28 and/or a recent history of weight loss should prompt further action and a referral for specialist attention. It should be borne in mind that the COPD population is at high risk of lung cancer and that weight loss could be an early non-specific manifestation of this.

# Treatment of nutritional depletion in COPD

Studies evaluating various nutritional interventions in COPD show that:

- Intense nutritional supplementation and weight gain is associated with better outcomes, although lung function does not improve

- Nutritional supplements given ad libitum in an unsupervised fashion produce no improvement in body weight; this is often because patients take the supplements but decrease their routine intake at meal times

- Anabolic steroids have shown some benefits in clinical trials but their role in the day-to-day management of these patients, with significant cardiovascular co-morbidity, remains unclear

- Dietary interventions, including supplements, provided in a pulmonary rehabilitation programme together with exercise therapy are more likely to be successful than just prescription of nutritional supplements.

*Table 6* summarises the various practical aspects of the management of nutritional issues in COPD.

**Table 6.** Management of nutritional issues in COPD

---

All COPD patients should have height and weight measured at baseline and BMI computed

History of weight loss should be explicitly sought from all COPD patients with moderate to severe disease

Lung cancer is an important cause of weight loss in COPD patients and a chest X-ray is a mandatory investigation in those losing weight

Patients with a BMI of < 20 or > 28 might benefit from nutritional interventions and consideration must be given for referring these patients for specialist advice

Nutritional supplements are better prescribed as part of a comprehensive programme including exercise therapy and in a considered and calculated manner under specialist supervision; prescription of proprietary supplements *ad libitum* without a proper evaluation of total energy intake and energy balance is not recommended.

---

## Depression and anxiety in COPD

Given the considerable limitations that COPD imposes on the lifestyle of patients, it is not surprising that the illness is associated with some mental health problems. Studies on the subject, however, show a surprisingly variable picture with incidence rates for depression ranging from 6–42% in a cohort of patients with COPD. The differences are explained in part by methodological differences in the studies (for example, cross-sectional or longitudinal; type of questionnaire used) and the severity of the disease in the patient groups studied. However, the studies suggest that:

- patients with severe COPD are at least 2.5-times at greater risk of suffering from a depressive illness than their healthy age- and gender-matched peers

- incidence of depression tends to be higher in those with hypoxia ($SaO_2$ < 92%) and severe dyspnoea

- depressed COPD patients also are more prone to exhibit features of anxiety

- depressed COPD patients also suffer a higher rate of hospitalisation for their illness and tend to stay in hospital longer.

The questionnaires used to identify depression in these studies are many, and often not validated in the COPD patient group, but it would appear that in practice any validated questionnaire or scoring system that the practitioner is familiar with and applies widely in other areas is likely to be as valid in COPD.

## Management of depression and anxiety in COPD

Although pharmacological treatments are effective in treating depression in patients with COPD, psychological treatments for anxiety have not been useful and are not recommended routinely. Among the pharmacological agents studied in COPD, nortriptyline is effective in improving the mood in depressed and anxious COPD patients. A study of fluoxetine showed that uptake of the antidepressant and concordance with therapy was poor in the absence of a clear explanation of the aims and rationale for mood-altering medication. Oxygen therapy when prescribed as per recommended criteria is also associated with a reduction in anxiety scores.

Therefore, to summarise:

- co-existent depression and anxiety must be actively sought in patients with moderate to severe COPD

- any of the conventional scoring systems used to diagnose the conditions that the primary care physician is familiar with may be used

- patients with severe disease, disabling dyspnoea and those with hypoxia (SaO2 < 92%) are more prone to depression; patients who are depressed are more likely to be anxious

- specific therapy for depression and anxiety is likely to be useful but must be discussed with the patient; concordance with antidepressant therapy exhibited without an informed discussion is very poor.

- oxygen therapy when prescribed and used as per established criteria is associated with an improvement in anxiety scores.

## Conclusions

Although COPD is an illness that affects the respiratory system, various systemic effects are evident in the more advanced stages of the condition. Depletion of muscle mass and weight loss, which occur even in patients with moderately severe disease, is associated with increased morbidity and mortality. Routine measurement of height and weight and calculation of BMI at diagnosis together with seeking of a specific history of weight loss at each consultation will enable early recognition of the 'at-risk' COPD patient. Lung cancer is an important cause of weight loss in COPD patients and a chest X-ray is a mandatory investigation in the management of COPD patientswith weight loss. Symptoms of anxiety and depression, which are commoner in COPD patients, particularly those who are hypoxic, severely dyspnoiec or have been hospitalised for their illness, must be actively sought using valid tools; for conventional pharmacotherapy to be successful it must be supplemented by adequate explanation of the need for problems of anxiety and depression to be treated separately in addition to COPD.

## What could I do?

- Recognise COPD as a systemic disease.

- Measure height and weight and calculate BMI at diagnosis; in patients with moderate and severe disease, ask for history of weight loss and measure weight at every review.

- Remember lung cancer as a cause of weight loss.

- Refer patients with abnormal BMI for specialist care, or dietetics advice.

- Identify and treat depression and anxiety.

## Further reading

Crockett, A.J., Cranston, J.M,, Moss, J.R. and Alpers, J.H. (2002) The impact of anxiety, depression and living alone in chronic obstructive pulmonary disease. *Qual. Life Res.*, **11**:309–316.

Ferriera, I.M., Brooks, D., Lacasse, Y., Goldstein, R.S. and White, J. (2003) Nutritional supplementation for stable chronic obstructive pulmonary disease (Cochrane Review). The Cochrane Library, Oxford: *Update software 2003*; Issue 3.

Managing stable COPD in chronic obstructive disease. National Clinical Guideline on management of chronic obstructive pulmonary disease in adults in primary and secondary care (2004) *Thorax*, **59**(suppl 1):107–116.

# Chapter 5

## Smoking Cessation

**In this chapter:**

Smoking is firmly identified as the greatest preventable cause of both mortality and morbidity in both the developed world and increasingly in the underdeveloped world.

It is clearly implicated in the development of COPD amongst other diseases and although the dangers of tobacco consumption are now well known and smoking has steadily declined over the last 20 years, there has recently been a slight increase among young people and especially women.

As COPD is for most patients essentially preventable, smoking cessation is one of the most significant interventions that health care practitioners can make.

With the introduction of tobacco into Britain in the 16th century, this wondrous product was widely believed to cure, amongst other things, ulcers, labour pains, cancer and asthma. It is now perhaps the most commonly used drug in the world. Not until the work of Doll *et al* in the 1950s were the effects of smoking understood. These studies followed a cohort of smoker and non-smoker doctors over 40 years but the effects of smoking were recognised early on in the study. As a result of these early published findings many doctors gave up smoking, but the message was slower to reach others. Despite what we know about the ill effects of smoking around 13 million adults in the UK are current smokers, with an estimated 82% of these having taken up the habit as a teenager. The reasons that teenagers take up smoking are varied and some are shown in *Table 7*.

Although the majority of smokers know that it is harmful, and an estimated one in three want to stop at any one time, over half of these smokers will eventually be killed by their habit. Unfortunately, few of those who start to smoke actually believe they will become addicted, but with an addictive pull estimated to be over 10-times more powerful than heroin, few are able to 'kick the habit' once they start. In the UK smoking is the single most preventable cause of premature death and disability. Smoking cessation is therefore the single most important health intervention that any health care professional can undertake

## Why is smoking addictive?

Cigarettes contain over 4000 chemicals including tar, arsenic, acetone, nicotine, cyanide and carbon monoxide among the more commonly recognised ones. Although many of these substances are harmful in their own right (tar, for example, has over 60 carcinogenic elements), it is only the nicotine in the cigarette that is seen to be addictive. Following inhalation of cigarette smoke, nicotine is absorbed through the lung lining and high concentrations reach the brain in 7–10 s, which is faster than if the nicotine was injected intravenously.

**Table 7.** Factors associated with the likelihood of childhood smoking

| | |
|---|---|
| ■ Low educational attainment | ■ Peer pressure |
| ■ Living with parents who smoke | ■ Weight control in young girls |
| ■ Living with siblings who smoke | ■ Low socio-economic status |

This gives an almost instant hit that is recognised as an important factor in causing dependency, and is hard to replicate with many of the nicotine replacement therapies currently on the market to help in smoking cessation. As nicotine levels start to fall, smokers experience withdrawal symptoms, including cravings, irritability, restlessness and lack of concentration, and to avoid these feelings the smoker lights up another cigarette. During the course of the day levels dip but analysis of plasma nicotine levels shows that they do not return to early morning levels.

Smokers rationalise that smoking gives them certain psychological benefits, mainly from the alterations in mood experienced, although many laboratory experiments have failed to find evidence of any mood-enhancing benefits from cigarette inhalation.

## Smoking and COPD

Although smoking is the cause of many diseases it has direct implications for the development of COPD. Whereas 90% of patients with COPD will have been or are current smokers, it is thought that only around 25% of smokers will develop COPD, with the risk being higher the greater the amount of cigarettes smoked and the length of time for which the person has smoked. This is often estimated in pack years, which is an accepted standardised concept for determining exposure to cigarette smoking *(see Fig. 16)*. Although it can be perceived that 75% smokers will not develop COPD they are, of course, still likely to develop another smoking-related disease and this figure could be an underestimate because of smokers developing other smoking-related diseases that may be their primary diagnosis. In addition to the development of COPD, smokers are also at risk of heart disease, vascular disease and cancer.

**Figure 16.** Estimating pack years

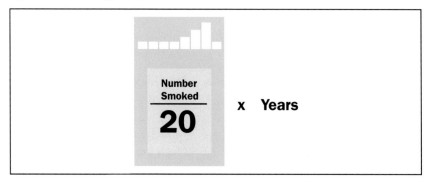

The evidence for the development of COPD through passive smoking is far weaker than that for active smoking; however, parental smoking is likely to cause increased respiratory illness in the first few years of life and this might be related to later development of COPD.

## The effects of smoking on the lung

Smoking causes damage to the lungs in three main ways:

- mucus hypersecretion

- alveolar destruction

- inflammatory changes in the airways.

### Mucus hypersecretion

In smokers there is an increase in the mucous secreting glands, the goblet cells, which increase in size and number secreting more and thicker mucous in an attempt to clear the noxious effects of smoking. As smoking also destroys the cilia in the lower respiratory tract, mucous is cleared ineffectively, causing difficulties with expectoration. This is characteristic of chronic bronchitis.

### Alveolar destruction

When inhaled particles reach the mucosal lining of the airways in healthy lungs they are destroyed by proteolytic enzymes released by phagocytes in the air-ways. However, these proteolytic enzymes can cause lung damage themselves, and producing inhibitors of these proteolytic enzymes protects the lungs, thus maintaining a delicate balance. If there are excessive proteolytic enzymes or a deficiency of inhibitors, then this balance is upset and the lung tissue can be destroyed, especially the alveolar walls. This causes emphysema. Smoking causes the inhalation of particles, which upsets this balance.

### Inflammatory changes in the airways

Neutrophils are the main inflammatory cells found in the airways. The number of phagocytes in the lung (particularly neutrophils) is increased in those who smoke. This causes an imbalance by increasing elastase load, eventually over-whelming the inhibitors trying to maintain a balance within the lung and ulti-mately leading to tissue damage.

These changes within the lung cause some of the commonly recognised effects of smoking (Table 8).

**Table 8.** Effects of cigarette smoking

| | |
|---|---|
| ■ Chronic cough | ■ Deeper voice |
| ■ Chronic sputum production | ■ Premature skin ageing |
| ■ Shortness of breath on exertion | ■ Nicotine stained fingers and hair |
| ■ Wheeze | |

Whereas patients might notice some of the more obvious side-effects of smoking, what they often do not appreciate is the effect on lung function. Smoking causes a more rapid decline in lung function than would occur naturally through the ageing process. That is probably why smokers notice shortness of breath as one of the cardinal symptoms; effectively the damage they have done to their lungs causes them to wear out more rapidly.

Smoking cessation is of substantial benefit to lung function, effectively slowing the more rapid decline in $FEV_1$ seen in smokers. It is estimated that the annual decline in $FEV_1$ in smokers can be reduced by about half if a smoker stops smoking. The benefits are felt for every age group, so it is never too late to stop *(Fig. 17)*.

## Smoking cessation

Smoking cessation advice is applicable to all patients but it should be the first intervention for patients with recognised mild airways obstruction. Smokers with early COPD who are successful in smoking cessation will have fewer respiratory symptoms within approximately 9 months and improvements in lung function *(Table 9)*

Some smokers especially those that have smoked for many years may be reluctant to stop smoking, as they believe that the damage they have done to their health is irreversible. Patients are unlikely to consider smoking cessation unless they can identify a tangible benefit from stopping. Once lung function has deteriorated it cannot be restored but the rate of deterioration can be reduced, as recognised by Fletcher and Peto in the 1970s. However, the truth is that for smokers it is never too late to stop, and the benefits of quitting start immediately *(Table 9)*.

**Figure 17.** The effect of smoking on lung function

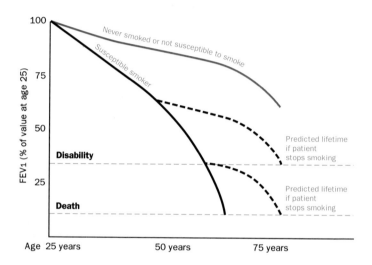

## Smoking cessation: a primary care issue

Health professionals often prefer to link smoking advice to smoking-related problems rather than routinely discussing smoking in every consultation as advised by guidelines, and some patients are unhappy about receiving advice before they are ready to give up. This approach might be ineffective, however, as symptoms often develop before any counselling is delivered, diminishing any health gain from advice on cessation.

Brief smoking cessation advice provided by GPs is simple and effective, with research showing that for every 40 patients given brief advice there will be one extra quitter where smokers are identified systematically and offered advice as a matter of routine (*Fig. 18*).

Therefore, for every 40 smokers seen in consultation who are not offered advice, one smoker who might otherwise have given up may continue to smoke. Every consultation is an opportunity to make an impact, and continued or follow-up advice can assist in sustaining quit-rates.

**Table 9.** The benefits of smoking cessation

| | |
|---|---|
| 20 mins | Blood pressure and pulse return to normal |
| | Circulation improves in feet and hands, making them warmer |
| 8 hours | Oxygen levels in the blood return to normal |
| | Chances of a heart attack start to fall |
| 24 hours | Carbon monoxide is eliminated from the body |
| | Mucus and other debris starts to clear from the lungs |
| 48 hours | Nicotine is no longer detectable in the body |
| | The ability to taste and smell improves |
| 72 hours | Breathing becomes easier as the bronchial tubes relax and recover |
| | Energy levels increase |
| 2 to 12 weeks | Circulation improves in the body so walking is easier |
| 3 to 9 months | Breathing problems such as cough, shortness of breath and wheeze show improvement with lung function increasing by about 5 – 10% |
| 5 years | Risk of heart attack falls to about half of that of a smoker |
| 10 years | *Risk of lung cancer falls to half of that of a smoker.* |
| | *Risk of heart attack similar to a never-smoker* |

More intensive individual counselling given in one or more face-to-face sessions by an experienced therapist outside of the general practice setting could be helpful for motivated quitters.

Smoking cessation is the most important factor in preventing disease progression in COPD. Although smoking cessation reduces the rate of lung decline in patients with COPD, there needs to be a constant message given to patients regarding smoking cessation. The message for patients is that the earlier they stop the less the disability in future life. Giving up smoking can be a cyclical decision process for many smokers, with many making more than one attempt to give up before stopping. Unfortunately long-term cessation rates are low. Many patients accept the early signs of smoking-related lung disease as inevitable and rationalise in the latter stages of the disease process that the damage has been done. Around 1% of smokers stop smoking of their own accord each year and simple reinforcement from a GP or practice nurse can increase this to around 3%. This may appear to be minimal but actually equates to 350,000 quitters per year.

**Figure 18.** Helping smokers to quit

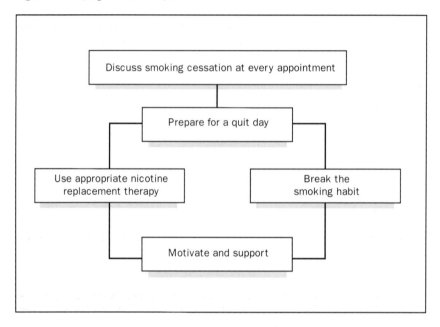

Effective smoking cessation includes education, advice and possibly pharmaco-logical support in the form of nicotine replacement therapy (NRT) or bupropion. Smoking cessation is clearly an essential and effective part of the management of COPD and needs to be a priority intervention for all health care professionals coming into contact with patients.

## Nicotine replacement therapy

Advice from the Department of Health in 1998 stated that tobacco addiction should be taken as seriously as other drug or alcohol addictions and that nicotine replacement therapy (NRT) should be available on prescription. This is important for lower-income groups where the effects of smoking appear to cause the highest rates of morbidity and mortality and who are least likely to consider smoking cessation or the benefits of NRT.

NRT is not a miraculous solution to smoking cessation for many reasons, but it does increase the chances of success for smokers giving up and has a proven efficacy. NRT minimises many of the withdrawal symptoms that patients experience following cessation, which are often the reason they restart. It also increases the likelihood of abstinence and is a useful smoking cessation strategy. NRT gives smokers the opportunity to break their nicotine addiction by gradually reducing the nicotine in the body while still getting nicotine.

NRT is available as:

- chewing gum

- transdermal (skin) patches

- inhalators

- nasal sprays

- sublingual tablets

and is required in a sufficient quantity for a sufficient amount of time to be effective.

## Nicotine gum

Nicotine gum releases nicotine when chewed and this allows the absorption of nicotine through the lining of the mouth. It comes in 2 or 4 mg doses and can be flavoured. Patients are advised to use a piece of gum when they would usually have a cigarette for up to 3 months and then to gradually reduce this. The gum should be chewed slowly, allowing the nicotine to be released. The 2 mg dose should be used at the start, with 4 mg being reserved for highly dependent smokers, or those who have failed with the lower dose. Although some smokers complain about the taste this apparently improves with use. Nicotine gum can be impaired by coffee or acidic beverages and oral and gastric side-effects have been reported.

## Nicotine patches

Nicotine patches release nicotine slowly over either 16 or 24h although there is no evidence that using the patch over 24h is better than 16h. As nicotine levels in smokers fall naturally overnight the 16h patch would seem to better replicate a 'normal' smoking habit. Patches maintain a steady level of nicotine in the body, giving plasma levels similar to those seen in heavy smokers. Users are advised to use the highest doses available at first, cutting these down gradually, and the patches come in various doses from 7mg to 22mg. Patches appear to be useful in those who smoked 15+ cigarettes a day.

## Nicorette inhalator

The Nicorette inhalator is a plastic mouthpiece into which a nicotine cartridge is placed. The smoker then sucks on the inhalator, replicating the hand-to-mouth habit of smoking and allowing nicotine to be absorbed in the oral mucosa. The nicotine is absorbed in the mouth and throat but does not reach the lungs.

## Nasal spray

Nicorette nasal spray contains a small bottle of nicotine solution that is sprayed into the nasal passages whenever there is a craving. Nicotine is absorbed rapidly into the nasal mucosa replicating cigarette absorption and could be useful for patients who are heavily addicted. The nasal spray is only available on private prescription and may irritate the nasal mucosa.

## Nicotine tablets

Sublingual nicotine tablets are dissolved under the tongue when cravings occur and can, for this reason, be useful for those who are heavily addicted to nicotine. The most common side-effects are nausea, dyspepsia and hiccup, which are all nicotine-related. An adequate dose, plus regular administration appears to work best.

## Combination therapy

There is some evidence that combining the nicotine patch with another form of NRT such as the inhalator or sublingual lozenges could be of benefit. It might, therefore, be considered in heavily dependent patients or those who have had no success with single NRT use.

NRT increases long term-quit rates by ~1.5 – 2-fold *(Table 10)*. NRT is most useful in those patients who are committed to stopping smoking and who usually have high nicotine dependency levels. This can be assessed by asking the patient how soon they have a cigarette after waking and also how many they smoke daily. The sooner a cigarette is smoked in the morning after waking the more likely the dependency (and similarly with cigarette consumption). The choice of NRT might involve consideration of patient need, tolerability and cost. Patches are most likely to be easier to use than gum or nasal spray in primary care settings, but there is no evidence that any one form of NRT is currently better than another. There is some evidence that a repeated course of NRT in patients who have relapsed after recent use of nicotine patches will result in a small additional probability of quitting

Patients might need to try different types of NRT before finding one that suits them. NRT is not a miraculous solution for smokers wishing to stop and no product works without the smoker wanting to give up.

**Table 10.** Smoking cessation success rates

| Success rates compared to no intervention | Quit rate after 6 months |
|---|---|
| Brief advice from a health care professional (3–10 min) | 2 – 3% |
| Advice and NRT | 6% |
| Advice, NRT and on-going support | 8 - 25% |

## Bupropion

Although NRT is the usual pharmacotherapy offered to patients, some people prefer a non-nicotine-based treatment. As depression appears to be more prevalent in smokers than in non-smokers, the theory that smoking cessation might precipitate depression, and that nicotine could have antidepressant effects gives us the rationale for using antidepressant therapy for smoking cessation. Two drugs used to treat depression, bupropion and nortriptyline, are recognised as useful for some smokers who are trying to quit

Bupropion (Zyban) reduces the effects of withdrawal symptoms and the desire to smoke by sensitising the nicotine receptors in the brain. Normally it is prescribed for a 2-month period at 300 mg/day with the smoker agreeing to quit on the eighth day of the course, once levels of bupropion have reached an adequate level in the body. Regular follow-up and support is advocated for patients using bupropion.

Bupropion appears to double the chance of smoking cessation. It might be helpful in those who do not find nicotine replacement useful. The drug is not prescribed to people with a history of seizure or with a history of bulimia, anorexia, hepatic cirrhosis, bipolar disorder or those on monoamine oxidase inhibitors. Bupropion is available on normal NHS reimbursable prescriptions

Trials of the tricyclic antidepressant nortriptyline suggest it also doubles quit-rates. The side-effects of this medicine include nausea and sedation and urinary retention and can be dangerous in overdose

**Table 11.** Susceptible populations

---

Both symptomatic and non-symptomatic smokers over 40 years of age

Ex-smokers over 40 years of age

Patients with frequent chest infections/chronic bronchitis

Patients with symptoms:    cough and/or wheeze
                           continual sputum production
                           complaints of dyspnoea

Asthma unresponsive to treatment (especially in those continuing to smoke)

---

## A practice approach

As smoking-related COPD is essentially preventable, one approach to reducing the morbidity and mortality from this disease could be to case-find in general practice and target all smokers. This proactive, and essentially preventative, approach to the disease at the early stages could be beneficial but not, however, very feasible. Nevertheless, the smoking history of every patient should be documented and updated regularly at every opportunity, with all patients continuing to smoke being encouraged to stop.

It might also be useful to think about susceptible populations and to target these at every opportunity (see Table 11).

What is apparent is that smoking results in heavy financial costs to the health care services and essentially preventable morbidity and mortality for patients. As smoking cessation is the only effective intervention that reduces the decline in lung function seen in COPD patients the most cost-effective intervention for all health care professionals is to be involved in smoking cessation. There are effective strategies and therapies to support patients with stopping smoking but the most important start is raising the issue with patients. Smoking cessation is therefore not somebody's business it is everybody's business.

## What could I do?

■ Give brief smoking cessation advice at every opportunity.

■ Target susceptible and high-risk populations.

■ Offer education, advice and, where appropriate, pharmacological support – NRT or buproprion.

■ Consider setting up a (nurse-led) smoking cessation service.

## Further reading

Abelin, T., Buehler, A., Muller, P., *et al.* (1989) Controlled trial of transdermal nicotine patch in tobacco withdrawal. *Lancet*, **I**:7–10.

Anthonisen, N.R., Connett, J.E., Kiley, J.P., Altose, M.D., Bailey, W.C., Buist, A.S., *et al.* (1994) Effects of smoking intervention and the use of as inhaled anticholinergic bronchodilator on the rate of decline of FEV1: The Lung Health Study. *JAMA*, **272**:1497–1505.

Barnes, P.J. (1999) *Managing Chronic Obstructive Pulmonary Disease*. Science Press.

Calverley, P.J. and Sondhi, S. (1998) The burden of obstructive lung disease in the UK-COPD and asthma. *Thorax*, **53**(suppl 4):A83.

Coleman, T. and Wilson, A. (2000) Anti-smoking advice from general practitioners: Is a population-based approach to advice-giving feasible? *Br. J. Gen. Pract.*, **50**:1001–1004.

Department of Health (1998) *Smoking Kills: a White Paper on Tobacco*. HMSO: London.

Doll, R., Peto, R., Wheatley, K., *et al.* (1994) Mortality in relation to smoking: 40 years' observations on male British doctors. *BMJ*, **309**:901–911.

Fletcher, C. and Peto, R. (1977) The natural history of chronic airflow obstruction. *BMJ*, **1**:1645–1648.

Gourlay, S.G. and McNeil, J.J. (1990) Antismoking products. *Med. J. Aust.*, **153**:699–707.

Henningfield, J.E., Fant, R.V. and Gopalan, L. (1998) Non-nicotine medications for smoking cessation. *J. Respir. Dis.*, **19**(suppl 8):S33–S42.

Hughes, J.R., Stead, L.F. and Lancaster, T. (2002) Antidepressants for smoking cessation (Cochrane Review). *The Cochrane Library*, Issue 4. Oxford: Update software.

Hurt, R.D., Sachs, D.P., Glover, E.D., *et al.* (1997) A comparison of sustained release bupropion and placebo for smoking cessation. *N. Engl. J. Med.*, **337**:1195–1202.

Kanner, R.E., Connett, J.E., Williams, D.E. and Buist, A.S. (1999) Effects of randomized assignment to a smoking cessation intervention and changes in smoking habits in smokers with early chronic obstructive pulmonary disease: The Lung Health Study. *Am. J. Med.*, **106**:410–416.

Killen, J.D., Fortmann, S.P., Newman, B. and Varady, A. (1990) Evaluation of a treatment approach combining nicotine gum with self-guided behavioural treatments for smoking relapse prevention. *J. Consult. Clin. Psychol.*, **58**:85–92.

Lancaster, T. and Stead, L.F. (2002) Individual behavioural counselling for smoking cessation (Cochrane Review). *The Cochrane Library*, Issue 4. Oxford: Update software.

Molyneux, A., Lewis, S., Leivers, U., *et al* (2003) Clinical trial comparing nicotine replacement therapy (NRT) plus brief counselling, brief counselling alone, and minimal intervention on smoking cessation in hospital inpatients. *Thorax*, **58**:484–488.

National Institutes of Health National Heart, Lung and Blood Institute (2001) *Global Initiative for Chronic Obstructive Lung Disease*. April 2001. Publication number 2701 NIHLB.

Pride, N.B. (2001) Smoking cessation: effects on symptoms, spirometry and future trends in COPD. *Thorax*, **56**(suppl 2):ii7–ii10

Silagy, C. and Stead, L.F. (2002) Physician advice for smoking cessation (Cochrane Review). *The Cochrane Library*, Issue 4. Oxford: Update software

Silagy, C., Mant, D., Fowler, G. and Lancaster, T. (2001) Nicotine replacement therapy for smoking cessation (Cochrane Review). *The Cochrane Library*, Issue 4. Oxford: Update software.

Wallstrom, M., Nilsson, F. and Hirsch, J.M. (2000) A randomized, double-blind, placebo-controlled clinical evaluation of a nicotine sublingual tablet in smoking cessation. *Addiction*, **95**:1161–1171.

West, R., McNeikl, A. and Raw, M. (2000) Smoking cessation guidelines for health professionals: an update. *Thorax*, **55**:987–999.

www.smokingcessation.co.uk/smokers/index.asp

# Chapter **6**

## Exacerbations of COPD in Primary Care

**In this chapter:**

An exacerbation of COPD is an episode of worsening symptoms especially dyspnoea, cough and sputum, as well as a variable degree of systemic effects.

They are often associated with fear, anxiety and depression.

Exacerbations in COPD can be minor events in mild disease, but in more severe cases they are the key determinant of health status and costs.

They are the main cause of hospitalisation and of death.

Effective management starts with patient education: recognising the symptoms and signs; and knowing what to do.

Exacerbations are important markers of disease progression. They are associated with reduced quality of life and prolonged morbidity and are responsible for 60% of the NHS costs of COPD. After a patient's first admission for COPD, there is only a 50% 2-year survival. Exacerbations demand effective early intervention and a thorough reappraisal of each patient after each exacerbation to optimise lung function and maintain physical fitness.

There is not an agreed definition of an exacerbation, but characteristic features include an increase in symptoms for more than 2 days, especially:

- breathlessness, often accompanied by wheezing and chest tightness

- cough

- sputum, which increases in volume and purulence.

Fever, malaise, insomnia, fatigue, anxiety and depression might occur. A high fever, chest pains and confusion indicate serious pathology and require urgent medical attention and re-evaluation of the diagnosis.

## Importance of exacerbations

### Human costs

Exacerbations are the biggest factor in determining quality of life in COPD. In those with mild disease, the worsening of symptoms might simply be an inconvenience, but in patients with severe disease an exacerbation is a terrifying ordeal. Patients dread the increase in breathlessness; exacerbations disrupt their lives, reduce functional ability and recovery is slow. Although most of the improvement occurs in a few weeks, it can take 6 months to fully recover. Often patients will not have recovered from the last exacerbation before the next one strikes. The frequency of exacerbations predicts the speed of decline in lung function.

One of the main problems during exacerbations is that patients take to bed. The combination of inactivity hypoxia, systemic inflammation, from the diseases process, and side-effects from steroid therapy causes major muscle strength deterioration, measurable within a few days; all too often this cannot be recovered. The damage of exacerbations can be limited by early intervention with pharmacotherapy, maintaining activity and preventative measures.

### Health care costs

Exacerbations are the main determinants of COPD costs mainly though hospital admissions, but also primary care visits and therapy costs.

## The causes of exacerbations

Exacerbations can be either mucoid or infective. In both there is an increase in inflammation, often with an increase in bacteria in the sputum. Mild attacks can be triggered by viruses, pollution or environmental irritants. This leads to an increase in cough, wheeze, bronchospasm, mucosal oedema and mucus production. Unlike those with healthy lungs, patients with COPD have a disrupted airway lining with poor ciliary function, damaged epithelium and scarred airways. Many have permanent colonisation with bacteria. When a virus attacks, bacterial overgrowth can follow, further adding to the inflammation.

Bacterial infection is reflected in sputum colour. The green discoloration is from neutrophil myeloperoxidase and indicates neutrophil numbers, bacterial load, and probably predicts response to antibiotics.

## Predictors of exacerbations

In general, the frequency and severity of exacerbation are associated with $FEV_1$. Other independent risk factors are:

- number and frequency of previous exacerbations

- current smoking

- low BMI ($< 18.5$)

- health status

- depression

- dyspnoea score

## Assessing the severity

It is essential to know the patient's condition before the attack, their pre-episode state, as changes in their symptoms and function are key factors. It is also important to look beyond the $FEV_1$ and consider the psychological and social factors, as well as other, co-existing pathologies such as cardiac failure or metabolic complications. Assessment in primary care should include how rapidly and how much symptoms have changed – breathlessness, cough, sputum as well as general well-being, psychological state, level of activity and ability to cope in their environment. The level of support and ability to respond to further deterioration is important.

Examination should include: pulse and respiratory rate; colour; temperature; hydration; and blood pressure. Signs of cardiac failure should be identified, as should focal signs in the chest. Other bedside tests can include spirometry or peak flow, pulse oximetry, and tests of cognitive function, e.g. the Mini-mental test.

**The danger signals are:**

### Breathlessness

Unable to speak in sentences, breathless at rest, too breathless to eat or drink sufficiently, paroxysmal nocturnal dyspnoea.

### Colour

Worsening central cyanosis; a change in level of hypoxia is more important than its absolute value. Pulse oximetry is useful and should be deployed more widely by emergency service in the community including GPs and nurses. (Hypoxia should not always be treated with oxygen; see below).

### Confusion

Any reduction in level of consciousness or increasing confusion is an indicator of a severe attack and demands urgent assessment in hospital including blood gases. Carbon dioxide retention often shows as tiredness or inability to concentrate and may be subtle in onset. A Mini-mental score of <8 suggests the need for admission.

### Chest pains

Although these can be innocent and often from intercostal muscle ischaemia, cardiac causes, pleurisy and pulmonary embolism should be excluded.

### High fever

This suggests pneumonia or serious bacterial infection and indicates the needs for admission (see Table 12 also for summary).

## Management of exacerbations

### Bronchodilators

Any increase in a patient's symptoms can be matched by increasing bronchodilator therapy, by frequency and/or dose. A change in delivery system or the addition of new agents might be necessary. Inhaler technique should be checked. Many patients have faith in nebulisers – their benefit can be psychological, related to larger doses of medicine, moisturising, or because patients do not need to coordinate their breathing to inhale the treatment. Those given nebulisers in an exacerbation should be reassessed afterwards (see Table 13).

**Table 12.** Danger signs in a COPD exacerbation

| Danger signs are: |
| --- |

any impairment of alertness, confusion

too breathless to speak in sentences

cyanosis, high fever and chest pains.

**These require urgent referral for:**

■ blood gas analysis, (to exclude $CO_2$ retention causing narcosis)

■ chest X-ray to exclude pneumonia, pneumothorax, etc.

■ VQ scan for some patients, to exclude pulmonary embolism.

After a severe exacerbation a thorough reappraisal of the patient is indicated and measures taken to reduce the chance of future attacks.

## Antibiotics

Antibiotics should probably be prescribed when the sputum becomes persistently discoloured, (some patients will have discoloured sputum first thing in the morning, which will be clear later in the day).

In patients with milder symptoms, failure to respond initially to antibiotics does not necessarily indicate the need for 'second line' antibiotic treatment. In more severe disease, ($FEV_1 < 50\%$ of predicted) patients who fail to respond to antibiotics have a high risk of hospitalisation. Resistant organisms such as *Pseudomonas* species are encountered more frequently. If the pathogen survives the antibiotics, there is a high risk of early relapse before full recovery. In more severe patients, especially with previous failed treatments or frequent antibiotic exposure, it is reasonable to consider a more expensive second line agent from the outset (see below for antibiotics used in second line treatment).

Second line antibiotics with evidence of benefit in COPD exacerbations include quinolones (ciprofloxin and ofloxacillin) amoxicillin-clavulanic acid combination, and tetracyclines (e.g. doxycycline; *see Table 14 below*).

**Table 13.** Three basic steps in the management of a COPD exacerbation

---

Increase bronchodilators (e.g. considering dose and frequency of use, number of drugs used and delivery system).

Oral steroids if failure to respond to bronchodilators.

Antibiotics, if sputum is purulent.

---

## Steroids

Oral steroids should be started promptly in any exacerbation when there is poor response to inhaled bronchodilators. Guidelines suggest prednisolone 30–40 mg daily for 10–14 days. There is no place for inhaled steroids in an acute attack of COPD, but they may have a role in preventing future episodes. Furthermore, subsequent attacks appear to be less frequent in those whose exacerbation has been treated with oral steroids.

## Other measures

### Information

Patients and their carers need to understand what steps to take with worsening symptoms, when to call for help, and when they are dealing with an emergency (self-management strategies are discussed in *Chapter 9*). Being able to recognise symptoms early and start treatment reduces morbidity. Phoning for help in daylight hours reduces the chance of admission to hospital.

### Reducing anxiety and panic

Approximately one-third of patients with severe COPD develop a panic/fear disorder. Many will hyperventilate when symptoms get worse. Rapid shallow breathing in patients with hyperinflated chests reduces the efficiency of breathing by increasing the physiological dead-space. Fatigue can quickly follow. Teaching patients about relaxation techniques including breathing slowly and deeply in the face of increasing dyspnoea is usually performed by physiotherapists and can be very helpful.

### Activity

Keeping active during exacerbations is critical to maintaining function. The combination of systemic inflammation and bed rest causes profound muscle wasting within a few days. Early rehabilitation during an attack speeds recovery.

**Table 14.** Antibiotics: Second line

| | |
|---|---|
| Quinolones | (evidence of benefit for ciprofloxin, ofloxancillin ) |
| Penicillin combination | (e.g. co-amoxiclav) |
| Tetracycline | (e.g. doxycycline) |

Often the patients are too ill to do much, but aids such as trolleys and rollators (wheeled frames capable of carrying oxygen) can help.

## Measures to prevent/limit damage in future attacks

A review should be undertaken after an exacerbation in patients with moderate to severe disease. It is an opportunity to consider referrals (e.g. to pulmonary rehabilitation, smoking cessation, oxygen and nebuliser assessments, and/or consultant review.)

There are three main components in a review:

### Education
Information about the nature of their disease and how to self-manage *(Chapter 9)* are often neglected. Early recognition of exacerbations is important, as is education about diet, relaxation and social support.

### Treatment optimisation (see Chapter 8 )
Optimising lung function in severe disease will improve symptoms, health status and future exacerbations. More expensive treatments might be cost-effective. Mucolytics may also have a place and evidence for their use in patients with chronic bronchitis is growing *(see Chapter 8).*

### Physical activity
Pulmonary rehabilitation *(Chapter 10)* reduces the impact of exacerbations and improves exercise tolerance and quality of life. It is important to encourage activity during an exacerbation as it helps to maintain fitness and promotes speedy recovery.

## Conclusions

Exacerbations in COPD may be minor events in patients with mild COPD but in severe disease they can be highly significant, both at the time of an exacerbation and in terms of future health status. They are poor prognostic indicators. Each one drags the sufferer down further and it can take months to recover. Frequent attacks cause an accelerated decline in lung function, exercise tolerance, mood and functional ability.

The main components are increased breathlessness, cough and sometimes sputum purulence. Early treatment reduces the severity and duration of exacerbations.

Breathlessness and cough are treated with increased bronchodilators and, if needed, oral steroids; antibiotics are indicated if sputum is discolored. A thorough review of patients with $FEV_1 < 50\%$ who have exacerbations is advised. The review should aim to optimise treatment: 'expensive' treatments can reduce the incidence of exacerbations and are likely to be cost-effective.

Patients should be taught to self-manage exacerbations, and should be encouraged to maintain their fitness with exercise. The costs to society and the patients of exacerbations can be enormous and optimum management is justified on medical, social and economic grounds.

### What could I do?

- Record the patient's condition prior to the exacerbation.

- Exclude co-existing pathologies.

- Evaluate danger signs.

- Refer to physiotherapy for relaxation techniques if hyperventilation is a problem.

- Use the opportunity of recovery from an exacerbation to optimise treatment and educate about future care.

# Further reading

Miravitlles, M (2002) Exacerbations of chronic obstructive pulmonary disease: when are bacteria important? *Eur. Respir. J.*, **36**:9s–19s.

Poole, P.J. and Black, P.N. (2003) Mucolytic agents for chronic bronchitis or chronic obstructive pulmonary disease. *Cochrane Database Systematic Reviews*, **2**:CD001287.

Rodriguez-Roisin, R. (2000) Toward a consensus definition for COPD exacerbations. *Chest*, **117**(suppl 2):398S–401S.

Seemungal, T.A., Donaldson, G.C., Paul, E.A., Bestall, J.C., Jeffries, D.J. and Wedzicha, J.A. (1998) Effect of exacerbation on quality of life in patients with chronic obstructive pulmonary disease. *Am. J. Respir. Crit. Care Med.*, **157**:1418–1422

Seemungal, T.A., Donaldson, G.C., Bhowmik, A., Jeffries, D.J. and Wedzicha, J.A (2000) Time course and recovery of exacerbations in patients with chronic obstructive pulmonary disease. *Am. J. Respir. Crit. Care Med.*, **161**:1608–1613.

Wedzicha, J.A. (2000) Oral corticosteroids for exacerbations of chronic obstructive pulmonary disease. *Thorax*, **55**(suppl 1):S23-27.

Wedzicha, J.A. (2002) Exacerbations: etiology and pathophysiologic mechanisms. *Chest*, **121**(suppl 5):136S–141S.

White, A.J., Gompertz, S. and Stockley, R.A. (2003) Chronic obstructive pulmonary disease. The aetiology of exacerbations of chronic obstructive pulmonary disease. *Thorax*, **58**:73–80.

# Chapter 7

## Management of Acute Exacerbations of COPD In Secondary Care

**In this chapter:**

Acute exacerbations of COPD (AECOPD) account for as many as 1 in 8 emergency medical admissions to hospitals in the UK; on average, COPD patients tend to stay in hospital longer (mean 9.1 days) than those admitted with other comparable cardiorespiratory conditions; readmission rates and mortality amongst patients hospitalised is very variable but high.

Maximal (usually nebulised) bronchodilators, controlled oxygen therapy, a short course (7–14 days) of corticosteroids and antibiotics are the key elements of routine hospital treatment of AECOPD.

Non-invasive ventilation (NIV) delivered via a face or nasal mask is a major advance in the management of hypercapnic respiratory failure due to AECOPD.

Mortality in COPD patients admitted to the intensive therapy unit (ITU) for invasive ventilation is no worse than in patients ventilated for non-COPD causes.

Appropriately resourced and staffed 'Hospital at home' and 'Assisted early discharge' services are successful in reducing the duration of hospital stay without adversely affecting outcome; the health economic implications of these developments are unclear.

The overwhelming majority of COPD patients (> 80%) die in hospital; advance directives, while available as an option for patients to participate in their care, are seldom brought to bear on the end of life clinical situation.

Acute exacerbations of COPD (AECOPD) were responsible for nearly 100 000 hospital admissions in the UK during 2001–2002. The condition is responsible for up to 1 in 8 emergency admissions to hospital medical departments in the country and, owing to the age and considerable co-morbidity in this patient population, constitutes a significant proportion of the work load of the medical services in secondary care. Although there is some evidence to suggest that care provided by a specialist respiratory team is better organised and superior in some respects to care provided by the generalists, the majority of COPD patients in hospital are tended by general medical teams with no specialist input. It is possible that the mean hospital stay following admission with an AECOPD, which is 9.1 days (median 6 days) and is longer than for comparable conditions such as an acute exacerbation of asthma, might be shorter for patients under the care of a respiratory specialist team with established links with primary care and access to intermediate care arrangements.

This chapter summarises the key aspects of the secondary care management of AECOPD. The definition and common causes of an exacerbation and the features that should prompt consideration of admission to a hospital are dealt with in the previous chapter.

## Initial assessment

Whereas in a small minority of patients hospitalised with a diagnosis of AECOPD the condition is neither acute nor an exacerbation of the condition, the vast majority are rather ill at presentation to hospital and require an immediate assessment. In particular, patients at risk of impending respiratory arrest should be identified promptly and appropriate measures, including assisted ventilation, if indicated, instituted without delay. Table 15 lists the basic elements of the initial assessment of a COPD patient admitted to hospital. It is worth noting that, in the course of transport into hospital, COPD patients might have received inappropriately high fractions of inspired oxygen therapy from fixed flow systems, aimed at keeping oxygen saturations high, and this might contribute to drowsiness and hypercapnia on admission. It is also important to bear in mind that pulse oximetry, which is widely used to monitor the adequacy of oxygenation, does not measure $CO_2$ levels; a patient with severe hypercapnia and in near-fatal respiratory failure can have acceptable ( > 90%) oxygen saturation levels with supplemental oxygen therapy. It is therefore mandatory that all patients with AECOPD admitted to hospital undergo arterial blood gas analysis at the earliest possible opportunity, with the fraction of inspired oxygen being noted.

**Table 15.** Assessment and investigation of patients hospitalised with COPD

---

ABC – Check if in, or at risk of, respiratory arrest. If not: full physical examination including vital signs (NB: respiratory rate); cyanosis and features of *cor pulmonale*

Pulse oximetry (NB: pulse oximetry does not provide a measure of carbon dioxide levels and high $SaO_2$ values on supplemental oxygen may be misleading)

Chest X-ray (focal consolidation indicative of pneumonia; pneumothorax; underlying lung cancer; cardiac co-morbidity)

ECG

Arterial blood gas analysis (inspired oxygen concentration to be noted) with particular reference to pH and $PaCO_2$ levels. Many patients with COPD have chronically raised arterial $CO_2$ levels; in these patients acidosis (pH < 7.35) is the guide to decompensation

Full blood count; urea and electrolytes

Sputum culture if sputum is purulent

---

Routine measurement of lung function by spirometry at the time of admission is not particularly useful in the setting of an AECOPD. Peak flow measurements, while performed routinely in many hospitals, are not crucial to the management of AECOPD and do not play the major role in management decisions as they do in patients hospitalised with an acute exacerbation of asthma.

## Differential diagnosis

In most cases the diagnosis of an AECOPD is obvious, but it is worth bearing in mind that in this patient population there is high prevalence of co-morbidity from cardiac and vascular disease, and therefore conditions including acute coronary syndromes, left ventricular failure and pulmonary thromboembolic disease merit consideration as the cause of acute breathlessness *(Table 16)*.

**Table 16.** Differential diagnosis of AECOPD

---

Left ventricular failure; acute coronary syndromes

Pneumonia

Pneumothorax

Lung cancer

Pulmonary thromboembolism (NB: examine for DVT)

Recurrent aspiration
(NB: previous stroke; neurological illnesses including Parkinson's disease)

---

# Hospital treatment of acute exacerbations of COPD

## Pharmacological management

Bronchodilators, systemic corticosteroids, controlled oxygen therapy and antibiotics are the main pharmacological agents used in the treatment of AECOPD.

## Inhaled bronchodilators

Short-acting β-agonists (salbutamol or terbutaline) improve breathlessness and are given every 2–4 h, or even more frequently initially. The evidence in favour of adding an anticholinergic agent when maximal bronchodilatation has been achieved with maximal doses of beta agonists is not particularly strong, but it is routine practice in most hospitals to give the patient a combination of a short-acting beta agonist and an anticholinergic agent (for e.g., salbutamol 2.5 mg plus ipratropium 500µg) via a nebuliser rather than either alone. Drug delivery via a nebuliser is preferred to a hand-held inhaler as breathless patients are less likely to coordinate inhalation or hold their breath for long enough to enable optimum deposition with an MDI; also, higher doses of drugs from an MDI requires an unacceptably large number of inhalations. For practical purposes, nebuliser equipment using a mouthpiece and a face-mask are comparable although, anti-cholinergic medication given via a nebuliser is preferably given via a mouthpiece as leakage around a mask may result in ocular side effects. In hypercapnic or acidotic patients compressed air, rather than oxygen, is used to drive the nebuliser for fear of worsening $CO_2$ retention *(see below)*.

Once the clinical condition has stabilised, patients should be changed to bronchodilators delivered through hand-held inhaler devices as soon as is possible. Clinical stability on the hand-held devices must be confirmed (at least 24 h in hospital on these) before discharge.

## Theophyllines

In addition to their bronchodilator effect, theophyllines are known to increase the respiratory drive and are used quite frequently in the hospital management of AECOPD. In patients who have not responded to maximal nebulised bronchodilator therapy, intravenous theophylline can improve the situation and circumvent the need for ventilatory support. Caution must be exercised in using intravenous theophyllines in the elderly (increased side-effects including dysrhythmias; in some hospitals it is routine practice to monitor continuously the cardiac rhythm of all patients on IV theophyllines), patients on polypharmacy (drug interactions particularly with commonly used antibiotics, erythromycin and quinolones which increase levels) and in patients already on the preparation as part of their maintenance therapy (tendency to toxicity). The therapeutic and toxic levels of theophylline are quite close and it is recommended that blood levels of the drug are monitored within 24 h of commencing treatment, and thereafter as clinically indicated.

## Corticosteroids

It is now accepted that systemic corticosteroids given during an acute exacerbation achieve a more rapid improvement in the patient's clinical condition and enable earlier recovery and discharge from hospital. While the debate about the optimum dose and duration of therapy continues, it is suggested that oral prednisolone at a dose of 30–40 mg/day is given for 7–14 days. There is no evidence to suggest that longer therapy is associated with better outcomes or that the parenteral route is better in those able to take oral medication. It is important that the steroids used for an acute exacerbation are discontinued after a stipulated period; there is, in the main, no reason to consider tapering the dose over a prolonged period of time and discontinuation of full doses of the drug after a 1–2-week course is not associated with features of adrenal suppression or relapse.

Inhaled or nebulised corticosteroids do not have a routine role in the management of AECOPD. High-dose inhaled steroids should be considered in patients with poor lung function ($FEV_1$ < 50% predicted) who have suffered more than two exacerbations in the last 12 months, in an attempt to reduce exacerbation rates and slow the decline in health related quality of life.

## Antibiotics

While it is likely that most acute exacerbations are caused by viral agents, a significant number are caused by bacteria. Patients whose exacerbations are not associated with the production of purulent sputum or features of infection (raised white cell count, C-reactive protein) might manage without antibiotics, but in the main most hospitalised patients receive antibiotic therapy. An aminopenicillin (amoxicillin), macrolide (erythromycin, clarithromycin or azithromycin) or a tetracycline are recommended as empirical first-line agents. In those who have already received any of these therapies in primary care, quinolones (ciprofloxacin, ofloxacin), including those with a wider spectrum of activity (moxifloxacin) may be considered. When patients are re-admitted with an AECOPD within a week of discharge from hospital, a diagnosis of nosocomial infection should be borne in mind and empirical therapy to cover gram negative organisms (e.g. third-generation cephalosporins, quinolones) considered.

Although it is likely that viral infections are a commoner cause of infective exacerbations of COPD, anti-viral agents do not play a major role in the management of AECOPD. There is some evidence that the use of anti-influenzal agents (zanamivir and oseltamivir) within 48h of onset of symptoms in patients with influenza improves the median time to symptom recovery and time taken to return to normal activity. However, their role is greatly limited by the need to start treatment very early in the illness, the difficulty in making a reliable diagnosis of influenza and the lack of evidence for their efficacy in COPD patients. It is therefore not currently recommended practice to prescribe these agents as routine in patients suspected of suffering from an acute exacerbation of COPD.

## Controlled oxygen

Almost all patients hospitalised with an AECOPD are hypoxic on admission ($PaO_2$ < 8 kPa). The aim of oxygen therapy is to prevent life-threatening hypoxia by keeping oxygen saturations over 90%. The propensity of high fractions of inspired oxygen to suppress the respiratory drive, worsen hypercapnia and cause further respiratory depression is well recognised, and is the basis for the advice for oxygen therapy to be given, not at highest possible fractions (as in asthma), but in a controlled fashion.

In practice, it is recommended that after performance of baseline blood gas analysis (noting the fraction of inspired oxygen), oxygen is given via a Venturi mask at 24–60% to keep the saturation over 90% and blood gas analysis is then repeated in 30–60 min. Increasing $CO_2$ levels and worsening pH should prompt lowering of the inspired oxygen fraction. Evidence of $CO_2$ retention or worsening acidosis, even at the minimum inspired oxygen fraction necessary to keep $SaO_2$ > 90%, should prompt immediate consideration of assisted ventilation, usually NIV (see below). Nasal cannulae are better tolerated by the patient than Venturi masks, and can be used in the more stable clinical state.

## Respiratory stimulants

Doxapram was widely used as a respiratory stimulant in patients with hyper-capnic respiratory failure not responding to maximal bronchodilator therapy, but its use has diminished considerably with the advent of NIV (see below). However, it might still have a role to play in a small minority of patients with hypercapnic respiratory failure refractory to maximal bronchodilator therapy who are either unwilling or unable to consider NIV and in whom intubation and ventilation is not appropriate.

## Other measures

- Diuretic therapy is useful in some patients with cor pulmonale and fluid retention precipitated by the exacerbation, although treatment of the underlying illness and hypoxia remain the more important elements of therapy. The potential for aggressive diuresis to result in dehydration and consequent renal failure, particularly in the elderly (who may also be on ACE inhibitors), must be borne in mind.

- Prophylactic anticoagulation (low molecular weight heparin) can be considered in patients who are likely to remain immobile and are at high risk of deep vein and pulmonary thromboembolic disease

- Physiotherapy is not of proven benefit in all patients and is not recommended routinely, but may be useful in patients with lobar atelectasis or those bringing up > 25 ml of sputum/day.

- Nutritional support: Patients with COPD often lose weight during exacerbations; due attention to calorific and protein nutritional intake may prevent this and the attendant adverse consequences of malnutrition.

## Assisted ventilation in AECOPD

The majority of COPD patients admitted to hospital will improve with maximal medical therapy but a significant minority will continue to deteriorate and require ventilatory support. Yet another group of patients will exhibit features of established or impending respiratory arrest even on arrival into hospital, prompting consideration of ventilatory support as an emergency intervention. Patients requiring endotracheal intubation and ventilatory support for COPD suffer a poor prognosis (11% mortality in hospital, with subsequent mortality at 20, 33 and 49% at 2 months, 6 months and 2 years). Nevertheless, the overall outlook does not lend support to the nihilistic attitude that is often brought to bear on the issue of ventilating patients with COPD, with studies suggesting that in-hospital outcomes for COPD patients ventilated in the intensive care unit (ICU) being no worse than those of comparable age and co-morbidity ventilated for other reasons. It is also evident from national observational studies that local service provisions and availability of expertise, rather than clearly laid-out clinical criteria, dictate the offer of ventilatory support to this group of patients.

If the patient's respiratory status deteriorates despite maximal medical therapy, respiratory support can be provided by:

- **Positive pressure ventilation:** where the device inflates the lung by the application of positive pressure into the airway [either non-invasively (NIV) by a tight fitting nasal or facial mask or invasively via a tube in the trachea] or,

- **Negative pressure ventilation:** where the lungs are inflated by negative pressure applied to the chest or abdominal wall (cuirass or tank ventilators). Negative pressure ventilators are not widely used (see Fig. 19).

## NIV

Arguably the single greatest advance in the hospital management of COPD in the last decade has been the use of NIV in the management of respiratory failure due to the condition. NIV differs from conventional ventilation in that whereas the latter involves the sedation and paralysis of the patient followed by the placement of an endotracheal tube to aid connection to a ventilatory apparatus, with NIV the patient–machine interface is not an endotracheal tube but a tight-fitting nasal or face mask (Fig. 20). The lack of need for tracheal intubation obviates the need for sedation and paralysis and all the attendant complications. Also, unlike invasive (conventional) ventilation, NIV does not require admission to the intensive therapy unit (ITU) and is often provided in

**Figure 19.** Methods of ventilatory support

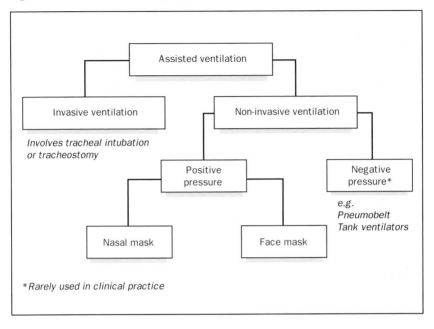

the setting of a 'high dependency area' in the general wards. Studies have now shown clearly that NIV, when used at an appropriately early stage of respiratory failure in the non-ITU setting, reduces not only intubation rates but also overall mortality rates. The indications and contra-indications, advantages and disadvantages of NIV compared with conventional ventilation are listed below (*see Table 17*).

It is now routine practice in most hospitals to offer NIV to COPD patients in respiratory failure refractory to maximal medical therapy. The usual indications for considering NIV are a respiratory rate of 25/min, a $PaCO_2$ >6 kPa and, most importantly, mild to moderate acidosis (pH 7.30–7.35). Institution of effective NIV is, in a majority of cases, followed by an improvement in hypercapnia and acidosis; gradual weaning (NIV continuously to intermittently during the day and through the night, to NIV at night only followed by complete withdrawal) of ventilatory support is usually possible over the following week, while continuing maximal medical therapy. An initial poor tolerance of NIV, low arterial pH (<7.3), malnutrition (low BMI), associated pneumonia,

**Table 17.** Invasive and non-invasive ventilation (NIV)

|  | NIV | Invasive positive pressure ventilation |
|---|---|---|
| **Principle** | Respiratory support delivered through a tight-fitting nasal or facial mask | Respiratory support delivered through an endotracheal tube or tracheostomy |
| **Advantages** | Non-invasive | Complete control of the airway |
|  | No need for sedation and paralysis | No concerns about patient cooperation |
|  | Patient awake; able to communicate, eat and drink | High, accurately controlled inspired fractions of oxygen can be given |
|  | Can be delivered in a general ward, Accident and Emergency Department setting |  |
| **Contra-indications** | Unconscious or uncooperative patient (absolute) | None unless there is a specific advance directive from the patient forbidding its use |
|  | Bulbar weakness (absolute) |  |
|  | Copious secretions (relative) |  |
| **Limitations** | Patient has to be conscious and cooperative | Need for sedation and paralysis |
|  | No control of airways – risk of aspiration | Weaning may pose ethical difficulties |
|  | Supplemental oxygen can be given, but in a less controlled fashion | Can be delivered only in the ICU setting |
|  | Tracheo-bronchial toilet not facilitated |  |
|  | Might induce claustrophobia |  |

excessive airway secretions and failure of pH and respiratory rate to improve within the first hour of instituting NIV, are associated with a poor outcome from NIV. In these circumstances a decision must be made on whether to escalate treatment to invasive ventilation, merely continue with maximal medical therapy, or scale down therapy to supportive care only.

## Invasive ventilation

Contrary to widely held opinion, in-hospital mortality in patients ventilated invasively for COPD is no higher than those ventilated for other conditions, when matched for co-morbidity. Nevertheless, endotracheal intubation and ventilation is an onerous undertaking and must not be undertaken without due consideration of all relevant issues, including the potential for successful recovery from the acute illness and, not least, the patient's own wishes, if known. *Table 18* shows the conventional indications for consideration of intubation and ventilation.

**Figure 20.** Patient on NIV with a face mask

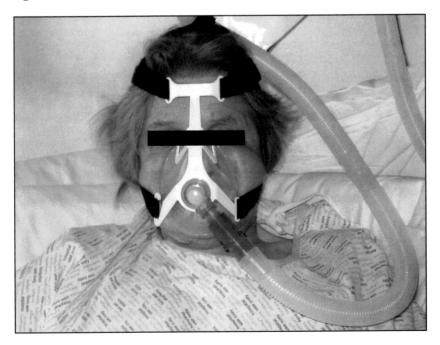

**Table 18.** Indications for consideration of endotracheal intubation and ventilation (invasive ventilation)

Respiratory arrest

Failure of NIV

Life threatening hypoxaemia (PaO$_2$ < 5.3 kPa or PaO$_2$/FIO$_2$ < 200mm Hg)

Severe acidosis (pH < 7.25) and hypercapnia (PaCO$_2$ > 8 kPa)

Haemodynamic instability

Multi-organ failure

Weaning from ventilatory support is often a difficult and protracted exercise in COPD. It is not uncommon for intubated and ventilated COPD patients to fail repeated attempts at weaning, with a tracheostomy being considered in view of the length of ventilatory support. NIV is sometimes used as part of a weaning strategy with the move from ITU to the general wards occurring via a step down through NIV and high dependency care.

Despite outcomes of ventilation being comparable with non-COPD conditions, overall in-hospital mortality for COPD patients ventilated invasively in the ITU is quite high (17–30%). Also, death after discharge, but within a year of admission to ITU, is particularly high in those with an FEV$_1$ of <30% predicted, those with non-respiratory co-morbidity, or those that were housebound before admission.

## Pre-discharge planning for COPD patients

Following the scaling down of treatment to baseline levels after achievement of clinical stability, it is important to ensure that the patient is on the intended 'discharge' therapy for at least 24–48h without deterioration. A visit from the Respiratory Specialist nursing team before discharge, although not mandatory, plays a vital role in ensuring that the patient understands the nature and scope of the treatment (in particular advice regarding cessation of steroids and antibiotics) and is using the inhaler device to best advantage. Re-admission rates among COPD vary considerably from one area and hospital to another, but a retrospective audit of 1400 patients in the UK admitted to hospital with AECOPD has shown that 34% were readmitted within 3 months. Good discharge planning and post-discharge care (see below) should reduce this unacceptably high readmission rate.

While hospitalisation with hypoxia and respiratory failure does not routinely indicate the need for consideration of long-term oxygen therapy (LTOT), admission to hospital does afford the opportunity to consider whether LTOT might be relevant in the long term. It may be appropriate to reassess some patients admitted with AECOPD 2–3 months after hospitalisation, when relative stability of blood gas levels may have been achieved, with a view to considering LTOT *(Chapter 11)*.

## 'Assisted discharge' and 'hospital at home' for COPD

The past decade has seen various developments aimed at circumventing the need for hospitalisation of patients with AECOPD. These developments have taken the form of:

■ **'Hospitals at Home'**, where treatments usually deployed in secondary care (nebulised bronchodilators, controlled oxygen and intravenous therapy) are made available in the patients' home by a suitably qualified and resourced team, usually of specially trained nurses and therapists, and

■ **'Assisted discharge schemes'**, where patients are discharged within a day or two of admission to hospital, with arrangements in place for a secondary care-based outreach service, with close liaison with primary care, providing close supervision and monitoring of treatment until recovery from the exacerbation.

While such schemes have been show to achieve outcomes that are no worse than in hospitalised patients, their scope and health economic benefits remain to be fully evaluated. However, in areas where such schemes exist, it would be to the advantage of the primary care physician to have access to such a service and be familiar with the relevant protocols.

## Following discharge from hospital

A primary care review of the discharged COPD patient is best undertaken within a week of discharge. *Table 19* lists some issues that could be addressed.

**Table 19.** Checklist of issues for primary care review of patients discharged from hospital following admission with an acute exacerbation of COPD

Planned duration of oral steroids and antibiotic therapy; when they are to be discontinued

Changes made to baseline therapy (e.g. addition of another bronchodilator including a long-acting bronchodilator; addition of an inhaled steroid or a combination of inhaled steroid and long-acting beta agonist; changes in inhaler device) and patient's understanding of these changes; inhaler technique

Smoking habits and consideration of measures to aid smoking cessation

Is there a review planned in secondary care? Any specific issues to be raised with secondary care (e.g. consideration for pulmonary rehabilitation and/or long-term oxygen therapy after clinical stability has been achieved)

In appropriate cases, a review of patient's experience of hospital stay and ventilation, as a prelude to a later discussion of advance directives

Are there baseline spirometry measurements in a stable state? If not, spirometry to be performed after stable state has been achieved

More than 80% of patients with COPD, including those with clear end-stage disease, die in hospital. Although the possibility of advance directives requesting end-of-life care to be provided in the home setting exists, there are currently no routine and robust mechanisms in primary or secondary care to enable patients to express and reliably communicate their wishes as regards their future care.

## Conclusions

Acute exacerbations of COPD account for a significant proportion of unscheduled care provided by hospital general medical services. An immediate assessment of the need for ventilatory support, controlled oxygen therapy, maximal bronchodilator treatment (including nebulised bronchodilators and intravenous theophylline), systemic steroids for 7–14 days and antibiotics (in patients with purulent sputum) are the key elements of treatment. Non-invasive ventilation (NIV) provided by a nasal or face mask has been the single greatest advance in the last decade in the management of AECOPD and has replaced tracheal intubation and ventilation as the main means of ventilatory support. Good discharge planning and a comprehensive review in primary care of the discharged COPD patient have a role to play in improving the quality of care provided for the COPD patient and in preventing re-admission. The period following discharge from hospital is an opportune moment to assess issues relating to smoking cessation, documentation of baseline lung function and aspects of long-term management including LTOT.

## What could I do?

■ Remember that severe, life-threatening hypercapnia can occur in the presence of normal oxygen saturation as measured by pulse oximetry.

■ Play a part in discharge planning, review after discharge and formulate a plan for further management.

■ Establish and maintain regular links with secondary care.

## Further reading

Davies, L., Angus, R.M. and Calverley, P.M.A. (1999) Oral corticosteroids in patients admitted to hospital with exacerbations of chronic obstructive pulmonary disease: a prospective randomized controlled trial. *Lancet*, **354**:456–450.

National Clinical Guideline on management of chronic obstructive pulmonary disease in adults in primary and secondary care [NICE Guidelines] (2004). *Thorax*, **59**(suppl 1):131–156.

Ram, F.S.F., Lightowler, J.V.J. and Wedzicha, J.A. (2003) Non-invasive positive pressure ventilation for treatment of respiratory failure due to exacerbations of chronic obstructive pulmonary disease (Cochrane review). *The Cochrane Library, Issue 3*. Oxford: Update Software.

Roberts, C.M., Lowe, D., Bucknall, C.E, Ryland, I., Kelly, Y. and Pearson, M.G. (2002) Clinical audit indicators of outcome following admission to hospital with acute exacerbations of chronic obstructive pulmonary disease. *Thorax*, **57**:137–141.

# Chapter 8

## Pharmacotherapy in COPD

**In this chapter:**

The pharmacological management of COPD can differ considerably from asthma.

Regular, long-term bronchodilation is a cornerstone of therapy.

Anticholinergic drugs may be particularly helpful.

Therapy will depend on disease severity; patients with severe disease are likely to benefit from the co-administration of several therapies.

Inhaled steroids should only be given to specific patients, and there should be an objective response to inhaled steroids.

For patients with more severe disease, inhaled steroid/long-acting β-agonist combination therapies have a role.

Therapeutic regimes must be individualised for each patient.

As in all therapeutic decision making, the choice of pharmacological agent should reflect an understanding of the pathology of the condition, the goals of treatment and safety. The international GOLD COPD guidelines define the condition as:

> *"a disease state characterised by airflow limitation that is not fully reversible. The airflow limitation is both progressive and associated with an abnormal inflammatory response of the lungs to noxious particles and gases."*

The definition implies there is some, limited, reversible component which is amenable to drug therapy with bronchodilators.

Avoidance of noxious stimuli, particularly cigarette smoking, is a cornerstone of COPD management. In terms of pharmacotherapy, medicines that modify the abnormal inflammatory response or indeed prevent disease progression will be most useful. To date, in COPD, attempts to identify such agents for clinical use have been unsuccessful. There are no known disease-modifying therapies for COPD. However, clinical experience with drug therapy, and indeed increasing numbers of clinical trial results, suggest that therapeutic interventions can offer improvements in a number of useful, patient subjective outcome measures. So our management of the condition should be directed not only at attempts to maximise objective management of lung function (as measured by spirometry), but also to make our patients feel better and lead as active a life as possible by reducing symptoms, improving exercise tolerance, reducing the frequency and severity of exacerbations and improving their overall quality of life.

Patients with COPD tend to be elderly and have concomitant diseases. This can lead to problems with complex medication, confusion, forgetfulness and poor adherence. Some patients, particularly those with arthritis, might have problems with manual dexterity and may find the manipulation required to use inhaler devices (and indeed tablet packs or bottles) a major obstacle. As therapeutic regimes become more complex, the possibility for drug interactions also increases.

But these problems are not unique to the management of COPD and form part of the standard, holistic, care of the patient. The rest of this chapter deals with the therapies and pharmacological strategies commonly used in the management of COPD

## Route of administration

In primary care, almost all prescribing for COPD is by the inhaled or oral routes.

## Inhaled therapy

Inhaled therapy is usually considered the preferred route: a smaller quantity of drug is targeted at the site of the pathology, reducing the risk of systemic side-effects. As in asthma management, when inhaled therapy is to be prescribed, clinicians need to consider:

- the availability of particular compounds in particular devices

- the patient's dexterity (often a problem in COPD – elderly patients may have co-morbidity, for example arthritis)

- the patient's ability to coordinate breathing with the actuation of an inhaler device

- the patient's ability to generate sufficient inspiratory flow

- the potential for confusion in using a number of (possibly different) inhaler devices, with different drugs, to be used at different times or for different purposes

- cultural views

- compliance.

As cost is now a major consideration in prescribing, there is a drive to use the cheapest drug and device possible, usually a press-and-breathe metered dose inhaler (pMDI). Several studies have reported considerable problems with the effective use of these devices, particularly in the long term. In a clinical trial setting, or soon after instruction and reinforcement by a clinician, many patients use pMDIs satisfactorily, with or without a holding chamber. In real life, inhaler technique may decline to a totally unacceptable level. Although pMDIs may be considered theoretically as efficacious as any other device, in practice, for many patients, they are not a realistic long-term option and cannot be considered effective nor cost-effective. The most expensive inhaler is the one that is prescribed but never used, or used ineffectively.

## Oral therapy

Although an important part of the management of acute exacerbations of COPD, oral steroid therapy, usually prednisolone, is not recommended for long-term use. Only in exceptional circumstances (and probably under the supervision of a secondary care colleague) should this be seen. Then potential side-effects – osteoporosis, myopathy, cortisol suppression, skin thinning, bruising – almost certainly outweigh potential benefits in all but the most severe cases.

Theophyllines, which are not available in an inhalable form, are the only oral therapy commonly used in the long-term management of COPD in the UK.

## Nebulised therapy

It is not clear whether there is a scientific case for the use of nebulisers in the long-term management of COPD. Similar doses of drugs are available through hand-held devices. It has been hypothesised that the longer duration of contact of drug with lung tissue (10–20 min rather than a few seconds) might account for the benefit clearly seen by some patients. Nebulised therapy should generally be reserved for patients with severe COPD. It is likely that these patients will have some contact with secondary care services and perhaps also use long-term oxygen therapy. Nebulised therapy should therefore come under the remit of a specialist respiratory team, who are usually best placed to arrange appropriate supply, proper use and maintenance of the device.

# Therapeutic classes

Despite some exciting attempts at developing new classes of therapy for COPD, at present pharmacological options still fall into just two classes: the bronchodilators and inhaled glucocorticosteroids.

## Bronchodilators

Bronchodilators are a valuable and essential part of any therapeutic strategy for the management of COPD. As in asthma, a quick-acting inhaled bronchodilator is used on an as-needed basis by patients with COPD for symptom relief. Unlike asthma, however, regular bronchodilator monotherapy can, and perhaps should, be given. Prescribers should recognise the different pathologies and aims of management between the two conditions, emphasising again the importance of correct diagnosis. There is no benefit from early introduction of inhaled corticosteroids in COPD, unlike in asthma.

## Short-acting β-agonists

These include terbutaline and salbutamol (β2-specific) and are well known and frequently prescribed therapies. Sympathomimetic, they act on beta receptors in the smooth muscle of the lung and cause bronchodilation (more correctly, they reverse bronchoconstriction). They have no clinically meaningful effect on the inflammatory process. They are available in a variety of inhaler devices that are generally cheap. Because of their efficacy and tolerability, there are, in general, few concerns about their safety and little doubt about their efficacy as long as the device is used properly. Patients should use them on an 'as needed' basis, prophylactically before activity, and perhaps as a background, regular, four-times daily regime, even at moderate to high doses. When this stage of intervention is reached – the need for regular bronchodilation – alternative therapies are available and are probably better *(see below)*.

## Short-acting anticholinergics

Short-acting anticholinergics (principally ipratropium bromide) act independently of β-agonists through an entirely different mechanism, causing bronchodilation by inhibiting the parasympathetic nerve supply to smooth muscle. Their efficacy in COPD is superior to that in asthma and they usually provide effective bronchodilation. The relatively slow onset of action of ipratropium (about 30 min) somewhat limits its use as 'relief' medication; patients demand an observable response in a few minutes at the most. Ipratropium is often given four-times daily as background bronchodilation, but is now being superceded by a more effective and convenient long-acting anticholinergic, tiotropium bromide.

## Combined short-acting therapy

A combination of a quick-acting, short-acting β-agonist and a short acting anticholinergic, either separately or in the same inhaler (Combivent®), can provide the benefits of both drugs in an additive fashion, with recognisable quick relief of symptoms. However, as ipratropium can only be given four times a day, the combination cannot be used as frequently as salbutamol alone.

## Long-acting β2 agonists

Inhaled long-acting β-agonists, salmeterol and formoterol, have been shown to have benefits in the long-term management of COPD, in improving lung function, exercise capacity and symptoms. In clinical trials, they have shown variable effects on exacerbations and quality of life. Some larger, more recent studies do show these benefits. As well as causing smooth muscle relaxation and reducing hyperinflation they may have other benefits including improving ciliary function. Increasingly, they are used in combination inhalers that also contain a corticosteroid.

## Long-acting anticholinergics

Currently only one drug is available in this class: tiotropium bromide (Spiriva®). The use of a once-daily anticholinergic as part of a therapeutic regime is highly appealing and early results in the clinical setting are encouraging. Although its efficacy against placebo is proven in terms of improved lung function, reduction in breathlessness and reduction in exacerbations and its superiority to ipratropium established, the outcomes of trials of its use with other therapies in a 'real life' setting are awaited. *(see Fig. 22)*

**Figure 21.** What outcome measures to consider when assessing 'success' after a therapeutic intervention, and the length of time needed to draw a conclusion

| Outcome measures | Time to assessment |
|---|---|
| Symptoms | Minutes or days |
| Activity | Days |
| Quality of life | Weeks |
| Exacerbations | 1 year |
| Lung function | Several years |

## Oral theophyllines

Although a mainstay of therapy for many years, these drugs have always been limited in their use by their side-effects, drug interactions and a narrow therapeutic range. A requirement for blood monitoring for dose is troublesome for both patients and medical staff. In patients who are entirely unable to use inhalers, they can still be considered an option, but other safer, more effective (inhaled) therapies that are no less inconvenient are available. On balance, these advantages outweigh the principal benefit of oral theophyllines – that they are cheap.

## Inhaled corticosteroids

In the late 1990s, four large clinical trials observed the long-term use of inhaled corticosteroids in the management of COPD. These principally looked at the rate of decline of lung function over time – a marker of disease progression. Many researchers were perhaps surprised, and certainly disappointed, that inhaled steroids in reasonable doses failed to alter the natural course of the disease. It was concluded that inhaled steroids were of no benefit in mild COPD. Recently, a meta-analysis of these studies, with a reinterpretation of the data, suggests that inhaled steroids *do* limit disease progression. The controversy rages on.

Some benefits were noted, however, principally a reduction in the rate of exacerbations. It is now recommended that patients who either have an objective

($FEV_1$) response to a trial of corticosteroids (which may include patients with both COPD *and* co-existing asthma), or those with moderate–severe COPD ($FEV_1$ < 50% predicted) with frequent (two or more per year) exacerbations should be given these therapies. It is unclear what is the optimal dose of inhaled steroid for long-term use, weighing the risks and benefits, but trials would suggest reasonably high doses are required: 800–1200 µg of budesonide or 1000 µg of fluticasone per day, given twice daily. Prescribers should note that these steroids are not currently licensed for use in COPD in the UK, except when given as a constituent part of a combination therapy.

### Long-acting β2 agonist/corticosteroid combinations

There are currently two long-acting β-agonist/inhaled corticosteroid combinations available in the UK: Symbicort®, a combination of budesonide and formoterol; and Seretide®, which contains fluticasone and salmeterol. Both are well known to clinicians through their use in asthma, and both achieved a licence for use in COPD in 2003. As noted above, neither steroid component is licensed for use as a single agent for COPD.

Recent studies indicate, in general, benefits of the combination over each constituent part and, in general, the long-acting bronchodilator and steroid components separately against placebo. Different trial designs and patient population studied make it difficult to amalgamate conclusions, but it would appear that there is a consistent reduction in the exacerbation rate and improvements in symptoms and lung function. They are currently licensed for use in COPD at moderate–high doses: Symbicort® 400/12, one inhalation twice daily; and Seretide® 500 (Accuhaler only), one inhalation twice daily

### Mucolytics

After a long period of being non-reimbursable on NHS prescription in the UK, having been 'blacklisted', oral mucolytics are again available to UK prescribers and their patients. They have continued to be used widely in other countries. Systematic reviews of clinical trials of their use suggest benefits in terms of reductions in exacerbations, reduction in days with illness and improvement of symptoms. They should be considered in patients with chronic productive cough and continued in patients who have an improvement in their symptoms. Carbocisteine (Mucodyne) and mecysteine (Visclair) are available in the UK.

### Antidepressants

Living with a long-term disease that has considerable morbidity and where guilt ("it's self inflicted; I shouldn't have smoked") can play a large part, can result in a depressive illness of varying severity. In this situation, long-term

**Figure 22.** A proposed step-wise approach to therapy

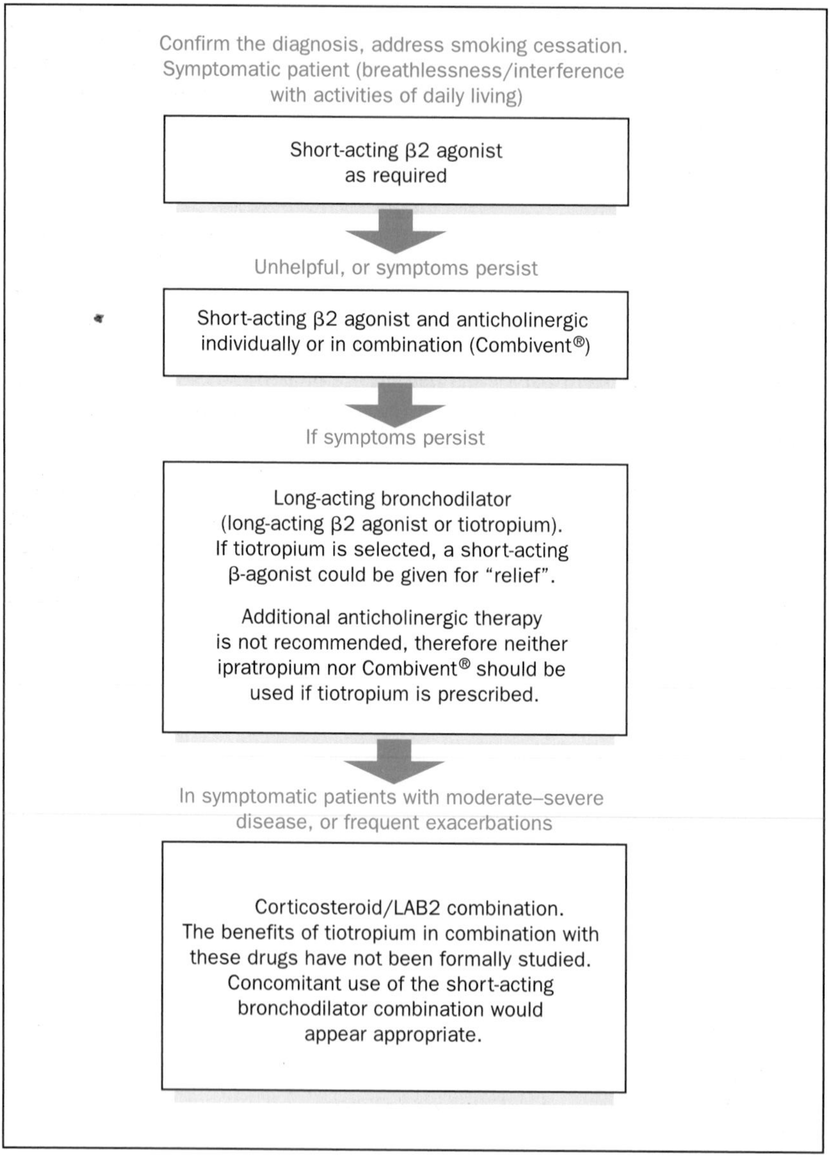

Confirm the diagnosis, address smoking cessation.
Symptomatic patient (breathlessness/interference
with activities of daily living)

Short-acting β2 agonist
as required

Unhelpful, or symptoms persist

Short-acting β2 agonist and anticholinergic
individually or in combination (Combivent®)

If symptoms persist

Long-acting bronchodilator
(long-acting β2 agonist or tiotropium).
If tiotropium is selected, a short-acting
β-agonist could be given for "relief".

Additional anticholinergic therapy
is not recommended, therefore neither
ipratropium nor Combivent® should be
used if tiotropium is prescribed.

In symptomatic patients with moderate–severe
disease, or frequent exacerbations

Corticosteroid/LAB2 combination.
The benefits of tiotropium in combination with
these drugs have not been formally studied.
Concomitant use of the short-acting
bronchodilator combination would
appear appropriate.

antidepressant therapy has a role. This approach also fits with the concept of COPD as a systemic disease, with effects on a number of organs and systems, not just the lungs. Antidepressants may, therefore, be prescribed as an adjunct therapy in COPD or as concurrent therapy for an intercurrent illness. Primary care clinicians are aware of the need not to manage any condition in isolation and, as always, a holistic approach needs to be taken.

## Predicting a response to therapy

A 'trial of therapy' is a well-established management tool. The concept of identifying a response to a short (2-week) course of prednisolone before instigating long-term steroid therapy is appealing. Unfortunately, this appears to be unhelpful in predicting a response to inhaled steroids. At present, given the available data, there seems no point in attempting to differentiate steroid responders from non-responders in 'pure' COPD, and the procedure can not be recommended. However, the use of inhaled corticosteroids must not be denied to patients who have co-existing asthma.

Similarly, although inhaled bronchodilators could be expected to improve a patient's lung function (when such an improvement is possible), a failure to improve spirometry readings does not necessarily mean that patients will not gain from these therapies in other ways: symptom control, improved exercise tolerance and quality of life. There is probably little point in relying on spirometry to indicate a benefit from a trial of therapy with a bronchodilator – better to ask the patient about subjective improvements.

---

### What could I do?

- Do not treat patients with COPD as if they had asthma.

- Prescribe effective, regular bronchodilation for all but patients with the mildest disease.

- Consider additional therapy as the need arises.

- Recognise, and assess, a wide range of outcome measures.

- Bear in mind that expensive therapies could be highly cost effective in patients with $FEV_1 < 50\%$ and exacerbations.

## Further reading

Lung health study research group. (2000) Effect of inhaled triamcinolone on the decline in pulmonary function in chronic obstructive pulmonary disease. *New Engl. J. Med.*, **343**:1902–1909.

Appleton, S., Smith, B., Veale, A. and Bara, A. (2003) Long-acting beta2-agonists for chronic obstructive pulmonary disease (Cochrane Review). *The Cochrane Library. Oxford:Update Software.*

Burge, P.S., Calverley, P.M.A., Jones, P.W., Spencer, S., Anderson, J.A. and Maslen, T.K. (2000) Randomised, double blind, placebo controlled study of fluticasone propionate in patients with moderate to severe chronic obstructive pulmonary disease: the ISOLDE trial. *BMJ*, **320**:1297–1303.

Calverley, P.M., Boonsawat, W., Cseke, Z., Zhong, N., Peterson, S. and Olsson, H. (2003) Maintenance therapy with budesonide and formoterol in chronic obstructive pulmonary disease. *Eur. Respir. J.*, **22**:912–919.

Calverley, P., Pauwels, R., Vestbo, J., Jones, P., Pride, N., Gulsvik, A., et al. (2003) Combined salmeterol and fluticasone in the treatment of chronic obstructive pulmonary disease: A randomised controlled trial. *Lancet*, **361**:449–456.

Donohue, J.F., van Noord, J.A., Bateman, E.D., Langley, S.J., Lee, A., Witek, T.J., *et al.* (2002) A 6-month, placebo controlled study comparing lung function and health status changes in COPD patients treated with tiotropium or salmeterol. *Chest*, **122**:47–55.

Mahler, D.A., Wire, P., Horstman, D., Chang, C.-N., Yates, J., Fischer, T., *et al.* (2002) Effectiveness of fluticasone propionate and salmeterol combination delivered via the Diskus device in the treatment of chronic obstructive pulmonary disease. *Am. J. Respir. Crit. Care Med.*, **166**:1084–1091.

Pauwels, R.A., Lofdahl, C.G., Laitinen, L.A., Schouten, J.P., Postma, D.S., Pride, N.B., *et al.* (1999) Long-term treatment with inhaled budesonide in persons with mild chronic obstructive pulmonary disease who continue smoking. *New Engl. J. Med.*, **340**:1948–1953.

Szafranski, W., Cukier, A., Ramirez, A., Menga, G., Sansores, R., Nahabedian, S., *et al.* (2003) Efficacy and safety of budesonide/formoterol in the management of chronic obstructive pulmonary disease. *Eur. Respir. J.*, **21**:74–81.

Vestbo, J., Sorensen, T., Lange, P., Brix, A., Torre, P. and Viskum, K. (1999) Long-term effect of inhaled budesonide in mild and moderate chronic obstructive pulmonary disease: a randomised controlled trial. *Lancet*, **353**:1819–1823.

# Chapter 9

## Self-Management Education in COPD

**In this chapter:**

Clear, measurable benefits have been described in studies using 'self-management' strategies in people with asthma, but not COPD.

Self-management education has many aspects.

Education about lifestyle changes, and knowledge of how to recognise and respond to a change in disease severity are the key elements of a self-management plan in COPD.

Self-management plans must be individualised.

Self management education in COPD may need to be combined with pulmonary rehabilitation to improve outcome.

Self-management education in *asthma* is now a fully accepted, if poorly implemented, part of asthma management. The situation with regard to COPD is much less clear. Self-management involves a patient making therapeutic, behavioural, lifestyle and environmental adjustments in accordance with advice that has been given to them in advance by a health professional adviser. The processes involved therefore include the giving of information, and the patient acquiring certain skills. This process will only alter outcomes if the interventions are of proven benefit and if the patient does indeed take appropriate action. The attractions of such an approach to patients are that they become more knowledgeable about their disease and their individual information 'wants' are met. Furthermore, the process acknowledges how unpleasant the feeling of 'not being in control' is for patients, who do not like being dependent on the doctor. The self-management approach thus recognises the emotions associated with uncertainty and dependency. In some health care systems, education and other aspects of management are offered increasingly by health professionals other than doctors, and this team approach is to be encouraged. However, in evaluating educational packages, we must not deflect attention from the fundamental importance of good communication within the doctor–patient consultation, even if part of that educational process takes place without the consultation, and is given by others.

In asthma, self-management education has been compared with routine care in over 36 randomised control trials. Systematic review of those studies shows that one can expect a 40% reduction in hospitalisation, 20% reduction in emergency department visits, and improvements in night-time symptoms and time off work and school. The situation with regards to COPD is that a similar systematic review showed that although patients were willing to undertake self-management education and did alter their behaviour, significant improvements in significant outcomes were not obtained. We therefore need to elicit why there are different results between asthma and COPD and try and determine which parts of self-management education might be most beneficial when approaching patients with COPD. It is also very important to remember that when talking of self-management education in this context, we are differentiating it from pulmonary rehabilitation. The latter involves several different interventions, which are described in *Chapter 10*. Whilst giving patients information about their disease and treatments is an important part of pulmonary rehabilitation, along with exercise training and advice regarding nutrition, it does not usually involve the patient being given very detailed self-management education or personal therapeutic action plans. The overall package of pulmonary rehabilitation undoubtedly has immense benefits for those with COPD, but the individual benefits of self-management education remain unclear.

# What might self-management education for COPD involve?

Any form of self-management education has to be individualised for the particular patient. We should also recognise that the patients' own fears and concerns need to be addressed. In severe COPD, depression is probably common and patients have understandable anxiety regarding the fear of exacerbations and the fear of 'suffocation'. There is also considerable stigma associated with this disease and feelings of guilt because most recognise that they should now, or should earlier, have stopped smoking. They might have unexpressed fears for the future and could have misconceptions about what that holds. Their goals need to be elicited; a goal such as being able to 'get out of the house' might be realised by a simple intervention such as ambulatory supplementary oxygen. These issues therefore need addressing, followed by self-management education.

Self management education has two major components:

■ lifestyle changes

■ treatment changes.

## Lifestyle changes

The lifestyle changes for somebody with COPD will largely involve avoiding further damage and enhancing the ability to cope with disability. It could therefore include any or all of the following advice:

■ Stop smoking and avoid smoky environments.

■ Use nicotine replacement therapies as appropriate and as advised.

■ Use effective breathing methods.

■ Use effective coughing methods.

■ Undertake your exercise programme as advised during your pulmonary rehabilitation course (remember that getting 'puffed' is not bad for you).

■ Eat a balanced diet including plenty of fresh fruit and vegetables and plenty of fluids. Avoid gas-forming foods such as broccoli, cabbage, onions, beans and sauerkraut. It is generally best to eat little and often. If eating makes you breathless, breathe supplementary oxygen while chewing or alternatively liquidise solids. Try high-energy food supplements if you are underweight, but do not make these an alternative to meals – they should be additional.

- Adjust your daily activities of living: sit down to do personal tasks such as washing or shaving, or to do household tasks such as washing up or preparing meals.

- Use a stool in the shower and a hairdryer to dry your feet or back.

- Have a flu vaccination every year and a pneumococcal vaccination every 5–10 years.

Although smoking cessation is undoubtedly of proven benefit, it will not lead to return of lung function to normal, but the subsequent age-related rate of decline will parallel that which it would have been if the patient had never smoked. The other lifestyle changes suggested above have not been subjected to formal systematic trial, but are nevertheless based on common sense and favourable feedback from patients.

## Treatment changes

When we compare the situation of self-management education in asthma with that in COPD, we see that in asthma there is overwhelming evidence that the intervention improves outcomes, whereas in the latter the situation is that it is of unproven benefit. (Note that some of the self-management education studies that have been published and show benefits actually included significant components of exercise training or pulmonary rehabilitation, which might have been the beneficial part of the intervention.)

The reasons why self-management education in COPD has not been associated with positive outcomes might include:

- inadequate number of trials

- poor trial design

- wrong outcomes measured

- wrong interventions used

- interventions do not work

- patients have not undertaken the appropriate changes

- lack of personalised written action plans.

It is not clear which of these possibilities are likely. There is evidence that patients do adopt the advice given by doctors and there have been at least 10 trials of self-management education in COPD which have been 'pure' in the sense that they have not also included exercise training. Only two of these studies have included the patient having a written action plan, and this component of self-management education has been shown to be one of the most important parts of self-management education in asthma. Of the two studies that have used written action plans in COPD, one included the patient being given a self-management action plan identical to that which we might give somebody with asthma, in that it encouraged the patient to increased their inhaled steroid and to take a course of steroid tablets if their condition deteriorated. This particular study (Gallefoss *et al.*, 1999, 2000) showed a limited benefit. The reason may be that such interventions are not effective in COPD. We know that steroid tablets can improve outcomes in exacerbations of COPD, but the magnitude of these changes is relatively small in that they slightly increase the rate of recovery of airway function and slightly shorten the duration of hospital stays. However, because the magnitude of that change is not tremendous, it is perhaps not surprising that a lesser use of steroids, for example doubling inhaled steroids, is ineffectual in treating COPD exacerbations (although inhaled steroids may prevent exacerbations). One of the other self-management education in COPD studies, from New Zealand (Watson *et al.*, 1997) used a COPD-specific action plan that encouraged the patient to take antibiotics when they deteriorated, along with steroid tablets. This study did show reductions in hospitalisation rates and in the duration of the exacerbation, but the numbers of patients in the study were too small for the results to be conclusive.

Most exacerbations of COPD are probably caused by viral infections and we do not as yet have appropriate or effective anti-viral agents for patients to self-administer at the time of a worsening of their condition. Bacterial cultures are often positive after the onset of exacerbation and trials have shown a small but definite benefit from the use of antibiotics. Their prescription is common clinical practice. It could be, therefore, that our COPD self-management action plan should instead contain action points such as follows:

■ If you notice more than two of the following situations, then you should start your reserve supply of antibiotics and complete the whole course:

- increasing shortness of breath

- increasing quantities of phlegm/sputum

- phlegm or sputum has turned persistently green.

■ If you feel more short of breath, you should increase your bronchodilator inhaler to two puffs every 3–4 h. If despite this, you are becoming increasingly breathless and you find that you are having to use your reliever inhalers more often (and optional... your peak flow readings, if you are making them, have fallen below....... ) you should start a course of steroid tablets (Prednisolone 5 mg tablets) taking six immediately and then repeating this dose every day for 7 days before reducing them according to your written advice.

■ If your ankles are more swollen than normal, or if you feel drowsy or have headaches when you awake in the morning, you should see your doctor urgently.

When patients who had been previously hospitalised with COPD were managed in a multi-centre trial with self management education of this type along with a home exercise programme, hospital admissions were reduced subsequently by 39% and Emergency Department attendance by 41%. How much benefit was attributable to each component is impossible to ascertain (Bourbeau *et al.*, 2003).

## Conclusions

Such written personalised COPD action plans, an example of which is shown in *Fig. 23*, now need to be subjected to clinical trials. We also need further trials to ascertain which component of a pulmonary rehabilitation programme is the most efficacious. Lack of proven benefit of self-management education in COPD on traditional outcomes should not obviate the need for good communication with these patients. Those with COPD often suffer stigma, depression, fear of exacerbations and feelings of hopelessness and depression. Giving appropriate lifestyle advice facilitates the discussion of the patients' goals and expectations and giving self-management advice returns a feeling of control to the patient. In time, the intervention to be utilised by patients, such as prompt administration of antiviral remedies, could make self-management education and the use of personal action plans as successful in COPD as they can be in asthma. The healthcare professional should elicit the patients' fears, address their concerns, be supportive and empathic and provide an optimal substrate for compliance with measures to reduce exacerbations, treat depression and encourage exercise.

**Figure 23.** An example of a pre-printed personal COPD action plan into which individualised advice can be written. Such advice includes both lifestyle advice but also advice regarding signs that might suggest impending exacerbations and ways in which treatment should be altered or started

## Department of Respiratory Medicine
## Charing Cross Hospital

# C.O.P.D. Self-management Card

Name: ................................................................

Hospital No.: ...........................................................

Chest Consultant: .......................................................

Respiratory Health Worker: ...........................................

# Self-management Plan

## Lifestyle changes

1. Stop smoking (and avoid smoky environments).

2. Use nicotine replacement therapies as appropriate as advised.

3. Use effective breathing methods.

4. Use effective coughing methods.

5. Undertake your exercise programme as advised during your pulmonary rehabilitation course. Remember: Getting 'puffed' isn't bad for you.

6. Eat a balanced diet: include plenty of fresh fruit and vegetables and drink plenty of fluids to help keep mucus thin. Avoid gas-forming foods such as broccoli, cabbage, onions, beans and sauerkraut. It is often best to eat little and often. If eating makes you breathless, use supplementary oxygen whilst chewing or liquidise solids. Try high energy foods if you are underweight.

7. Adjust daily activities of living. Sit down to do personal tasks such as washing or shaving or doing household tasks such as washing up or preparing meals.

8. Use a stool in the shower and use a hairdryer to dry feet or back.

9. Have flu vaccination every year and pneumovax every 5 to 10 years.

## Treatment changes

1. Take your .....................inhaler in the dose of 2 puffs, 4 times every day.

2. Take your .....................inhaler in the dose of 2 puffs, twice a day.

3. Take your .....................inhaler in the dose of 2 puffs, twice a day.

4. If you feel any more breathless you may take your .................. inhaler 2 puffs, every 3 to 4 hours to relieve symptoms.

5. If you get much more breathless or your peak flow readings if you are making them have fallen below ........., then you should increase your ................... inhaler to a dosage of ....... puffs....... times a day. If despite this you are becoming increasingly breathless and you find you are having to use your blue inhaler very often and your peak flow readings, if you are making them, have fallen below ............... you should start a course of steroid tablets by taking 6 tablets (5mg) immediately and repeat this dose every day for 7 days before stopping the tablets (or reducing them according to individualised advice).

6. If you notice more than two of the following situations then you should start your reserve supply of antibiotics and complete the whole course-
   • Increasingly short of breath
   • increasing quantities of phlegm/sputum
   • phlegm or sputum has turned persistently green

7. If your ankles are more swollen than normal you should see your doctor.

If despite all of these measures you still feel worse then you should ring your doctor on ...................................

## Oxygen

Use your oxygen as advised - either long-term or supplementary during exertion - know when to increase this and be aware of the importance of early morning confusion or headaches which might suggest that you are retaining your exhaust gas (carbon dioxide).

If you have been given a COPD Alert Card (because you have previously had Type II Respiratory failure) make sure that you show this to any doctor you see and to Ambulance Personnel.

## Further Information

If you want further information about your condition do ask your doctor or nurse, or you can contact -

**British Lung Foundation**

**73 - 75 Goswell Road,**

**London EC1V 7ER**

**Tel: 020 7688 5555**

**www.lunguk.org/**

# What could I do?

■ Give people with COPD advice and education about lifestyle as well as maximising pharmacological therapy.

■ Educate, then agree and support the increased use by patients of bronchodilators as their symptoms worsen.

■ Prescribe reserve supplies of antibiotics and corticosteroid tablets.

■ Agree when these medicines should be used.

■ Produce a written self-management plan.

## References and further reading

Bourbeau, J., Julien, M., Maltais, F., Rouleau, M., Beaupre, A., Begin, R. *et al.* (2003) Reduction of hospital utilization in patients with chronic obstructive pulmonary disease – a disease-specific self-management intervention. *Arch Intern Med,* **163**:585–591.

Gallefoss, F. and Bakke, P.S. (1999) How does patient education and self management among asthmatics and patients with chronic obstructive pulmonary disease affect medication? *Am. J. Respir. Crit. Care. Med.,* **160**:2000–2005.

Gallefoss, F. and Bakke, P.S. (2000) Impact of patient education and self management on morbidity in asthmatics and patients with chronic obstructive pulmonary disease. *Respir. Med.,* **94**:279–287.

Monninkhof, E., van der Valk, P., van der Palen, J., van Herwaarden, C., Partridge, M.R. and Zielhuis, G. (2003) Self-management education for patients with chronic obstructive pulmonary disease: a systematic review. *Thorax,* **58**:394–398.

Watson, P.B., Town, G.I., Holbrook, N., Dwan, C., Toop, L.J. and Drennan, C.J. (1997) Evaluation of a self-management plan for chronic obstructive pulmonary disease. *Eur. Respir. J.,* **10**:1267-71.

# Chapter 10

## Pulmonary
## Rehabilitation

**In this chapter:**

Pulmonary rehabilitation is becoming an increasingly important component in the management, care and treatment of patients with chronic lung disease.

Funding issues have often hampered the development of a programme that has a recognised benefit to patients disabled by their respiratory disease.

Successful pulmonary rehabilitation programmes combine programmes of exercise and education and often involve a range of health care professionals.

The location of the programme can be in either a primary or secondary care setting.

While the concept of pulmonary rehabilitation is increasingly being recognised as beneficial to our patients, its place in the treatment of COPD has been slow to be established. There are several reasons for this. First, although the concept of rehabilitation is not new and indeed is well recognised in cardiovascular disease, rehabilitation is seen as a means to return the patient to normality following acute episodes. Little attention has been given to the use of rehabilitation in chronic disease management. Second, the nihilistic viewpoint of COPD that has prevailed for many years has perpetuated the view that there is little that can be done for this group of patients, although this idea is slowly changing. The final reason is that pulmonary rehabilitation has running costs and the benefits to both patients and the health care economy have to be recognised in order for funding to follow.

## What is pulmonary rehabilitation?

Although there are a number of definitions of pulmonary rehabilitation one of the most widely used is that of the American Thoracic Society, which states that:

> *Pulmonary rehabilitation is a multi-disciplinary programme of care for patients with chronic respiratory impairment that is individually tailored and designed to optimise physical and social performance and autonomy.'*

Pulmonary rehabilitation is therefore an organised programme of exercise and education that is prescribed on an individual basis for patients hampered by symptoms of their respiratory diseases. It aims to improve both physical fitness and social well-being while giving the patient control over the disability and impairment caused by the lung disease and also over the handicap that results.

The aims of pulmonary rehabilitation are therefore to:

■ enhance functional performance

■ improve the patients' quality of life

■ promote physical independence

■ improve psychosocial well-being.

These aims taken together endeavour to restore the patient to the highest level of independent functioning.

## Why is it necessary for our patients?

The most common presenting symptom for patients with COPD is breathlessness, and this breathlessness is a symptom of the patients' underlying lung disease; the lungs are simply not working efficiently enough to give the patients sufficient oxygen, and in response to this patients restrict their activities, causing progressive deconditioning. Unfortunately patients then become trapped in a vicious circle further restricting their activities, which leads to breathlessness at even lower levels of exercise. The deconditioning process continues bringing with it other problems, such as social isolation and depression and anxiety (see Fig. 24).

Unfortunately most patients with COPD present with breathlessness only when it is having a significant effect on their lives. Although their breathlessness may be associated initially with physically demanding activities such as exercise, gardening or housework, patients often compensate for this by reducing their physical activity. Eventually the breathlessness might start to interfere with the patient's more basic activities of daily living and this could be the cue for them to seek help. As physical ability declines and activity is avoided, physical fitness declines in the same way as occurs in healthy individuals. The patient's condition steadily worsens as a result of breathlessness, now associated with both respiratory disease and reduced levels of fitness. As a patient becomes incapacitated, they can become socially isolated and, in some cases, depressed. Pulmonary rehabilitation aims to reverse this process.

**Figure 24.** The cycle of breathlessness

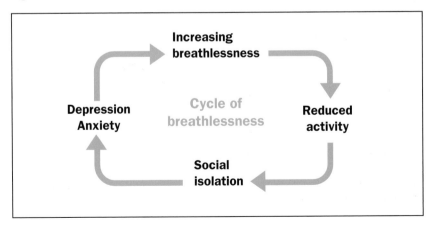

Another symptom that patients with COPD complain about is fatigue. This occurs because they are tired out by the work of breathing, because they are deconditioned through responding to breathlessness by limiting their activities and because of other problems such as poor sleep patterns. Fatigue can also increase feelings of depression and social isolation.

## Which patients benefit from pulmonary rehabilitation?

There is increasing evidence that patients with many levels of disease severity will benefit from pulmonary rehabilitation, although those that have the motivation to want to improve their lives are likely to do better. Whereas it is increasingly recognised that the severity of the lung function has very little correlation with an individual's perception and experience of breathlessness, rehabilitation programmes presume that any patient experiencing breathlessness that impacts on their lives is likely to benefit *(Table 20)*. Breathlessness is very much what the patient says it is and not easy to define purely on objective spirometric lung measurement. As a general rule patients at stage 3 and above on the MRC dyspnoea scale appear to benefit from pulmonary rehabilitation *(Table 21)*.

**Table 20.** Suitability for pulmonary rehabilitation

| No Barrier | Barriers |
| --- | --- |
| FEV1 | Co-morbidity |
| Age | Transport problems |
| Gender | Geographical location |
| Level of disability | Language difficulties |
| Oxygen dependent | Lack of motivation |
| Current smoker | |

**Table 21.** The MRC dyspnoea scale

| Grade | Degree of breathlessness related to activity |
| --- | --- |
| 1 | Not troubled by breathlessness usually, only with strenuous exercise |
| 2 | Short of breath when hurrying on the level or walking up a slight hill |
| 3 | Walks slower than contemporaries of the same age on the level because of breathlessness, or has to stop for breath when walking at own pace on the level |
| 4 | Stops for breath after walking about 100 yards or after a few minutes on the level |
| 5 | Too breathless to leave the house or breathless when dressing and undressing |

The MRC scale allows the patient to rate the degree of disability associated with their disease and also serves to give some indication of the patient's exercise tolerance.

Pulmonary rehabilitation should only be considered when medical management of the patient is optimal and their condition is clinically stable; therefore, optimal pharmacological management is important. Patients with severe disease are as likely to do well from the programme and patients requiring oxygen need not be excluded provided there are portable system for use in the classes.

Undoubtedly patients committed to completing the programme and wishing to improve on their disability are likely to do the best and are more likely to complete the course. It could be useful to take into account the patient viewpoint as to what they want when planning their programme *(Table 22)*.

**Table 22.** What patients might want

Increased mobility

Reduction in disability

Freedom from symptoms

Stable disease

Increased knowledge

A consistent approach to care

Control

## What should a programme entail?

Pulmonary rehabilitation traditionally consists of two elements:

- physical exercise

- an educational component.

Although these might be distinct components it appears that they complement each other.

## Physical exercise component

The evidence for rehabilitation points to benefits for patients through lower limb aerobic activity, for example cycling, stepping and walking. The benefits of upper limb exercise are not as evident, although low-intensity, peripheral muscle training has been shown to be beneficial. In determining the exercise level for each patient, exercise should be prescribed at around 60–80% of an individual's peak capacity, i.e. at a high enough level to provoke a physiological training response. There is some evidence to show that training at a higher intensity might be even more effective. To establish an individual's exercise tolerance a formal laboratory-based exercise test can be performed, or a field exercise test, e.g. a corridor-walking test *(see Fig. 25)*.

All exercise should be prescribed individually and this possibly explains why patients do not benefit as much from exercise classes where exercise is on a group basis.

## Education component

The educational component of pulmonary rehabilitation might vary between courses but evidence seems to suggest that a multi-professional approach works well *(Fig. 26)*.

**Figure 25.** A corridor-walking test

**Figure 26.** The various members of the multi-professional team

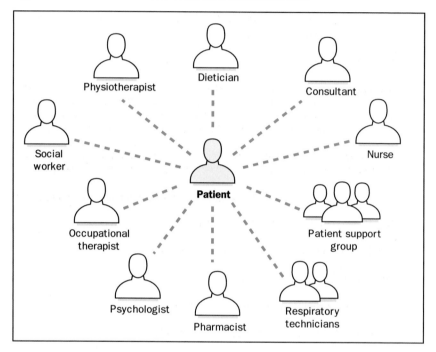

However, it is recognised that not all these professionals might be available for the programme, and programmes undertaken with relatively few health care professionals are still beneficial and effective.

Patient education in pulmonary rehabilitation covers a wide range of subjects delivered both by informal and more practical sessions The educational component of pulmonary rehabilitation, however, does not appear to be effective on its own without the exercise component.

Before commencing the course, the patient's exercise tolerance, health status, psychological status and ability to complete daily living activities should be assessed. There are a variety of tools available to assist in this process. Spirometry can be performed to identify the patient's degree of impairment although, as COPD is by definition irreversible, it would not be expected to improve after rehabilitation. Outcome measures for pulmonary rehabilitation may include improvements both in exercise tolerance and health status.

Exercise tolerance can be measured by:

■ The 6-minute walking test where patients are instructed to cover as much ground as possible in 6 min

■ The shuttle walking test, which measures maximum capacity:

**the incremental shuttle walking test** is a paced and incremental test where patients walk between two cones 10 m apart at speeds dictated by sounds from a tape cassette. The speed of walking is increased every minute and stresses the patient to maximal performance, which is symptom-limited;

**the endurance shuttle walking test** sets the workload at a constant pace and the patient walks at this pace until their symptoms limit their performance.

Health status can be measured by a variety of validated questionnaires such as:

■ The St George's Respiratory Questionnaire

■ The Canadian Occupational Performance Measure

■ Short Form 36 Health Survey (SF 36)

■ The Chronic Respiratory Disease Questionnaire

■ The Hospital Anxiety and Depression Scale (HADS).

It is important to remember that health status has only a weak correlation with functional capacity.

# What can the various members bring to the educational component of rehabilitation?

A range of health care professionals can be involved in the rehabilitation programme and will have a range of knowledge and skills to offer.

## Consultant/GP

Traditionally a respiratory physician has acted as the clinical lead for the programme. However, this is probably not as important as having a consultant or GP with an interest in respiratory disease to assess the patient for suitability to undertake the programme. The physician/GP could contribute to the programme by offering advice on the basic anatomy, physiology and treatment of COPD.

## Physiotherapist

Some programmes are almost wholly run by physiotherapists. They are certainly likely to oversee the exercise component. Other roles for physiotherapists might be the management of breathlessness, breathing control and effective chest clearance.

## Occupational therapist

The occupational therapy input to the programme might involve goal setting, pacing strategies and relaxation techniques. This is also a good opportunity to look at aids that could be useful in assisting patients with their activities of daily living. These could include items such as stair rails, walking frames and perching stools or smaller devices such as helping hands to help patients pick up items without having to bend.

## Pharmacist

Although optimal medication management should be undertaken before the patient commences their rehabilitation, there might be some patients who do not fully understand why and what they are taking and how to take it. In addition to the medication that patients may take for their respiratory disease they might also take a number of medications for other co-morbidities. Patients might find it useful to receive information both on medication usage, side-effects and devices.

## Nurse

Nurses can be involved in the overall organisation of the rehabilitation programme and could also talk about recognising exacerbations, when to seek help hospital care and, in some cases, may talk about psychological issues in respiratory disease.

## Dietician

Many patients with COPD can benefit from dietetic advice either to manage obesity (usually those with BMI > 30) or to improve on low body weight (BMI < 20; *see Table 23*). Patients with advanced COPD can find it difficult to maintain their weight and there is evidence that these patients have a poorer prognostic outcome. Patients with a high body weight might benefit from advice on how to reduce their weight as carrying extra weight can increase breathlessness. For those with a low body weight, advice could be given on foods that have a high calorific value that are also easy to consume and patients may be advised to eat little and often.

**Table 23.** Body Mass Index (BMI)

$$BMI = \frac{\text{Weight (in kg)}}{\text{Height}_2 \text{ (in metres)}}$$

| BMI | Nutritional status |
|-----|-------------------|
| < 16 | Severe malnourishment |
| 16–18.5 | Moderate malnourishment |
| 18.5–21 | At risk |
| 21–25 | Ideal |
| 25–30 | Moderate obesity |
| > 30 | Severe obesity |

## Respiratory technicians

The input of the respiratory technician could include explaining lung function tests, using and servicing of nebulisers, or advice on oxygen therapy and travel.

## Psychologists

Few programmes currently have psychology input, although many of the interventions that they can offer are applicable to patients with chronic disease. Interventions may include cognitive behavioural therapy, goal and target setting and stress management. It is clear that psychological issues affect patients and can impact on their physiological functioning.

Any of the members of the multi-professional team might be involved in the issue of smoking cessation, which is an important message in COPD care. Issues such as after-care and benefits advice might also be part of the educational component.

## Is rehabilitation a primary or secondary care issue?

Pulmonary rehabilitation evolved in the hospital setting; however, it appears that the location of the course is of less importance than the actual content. Both locations have positive and negative points. In primary care the location might be easier for patients to get to, but the facilities and personnel might be more limited than in secondary care. What is clear is that in order to demonstrate a physiological training effect, patients need to exercise:

- for between 4 and 12 weeks

- for a minimum of twice a week

- for around 20–30 min at a time.

## After-care

What happens with patients after completing their programme is probably as important as what takes place during the course. Those patients that take on the ethos of pulmonary rehabilitation and continue to exercise do far better than patients who complete the course and then return to a sedentary lifestyle. Where possible patients should be encouraged to maintain their levels of fitness and short top-up programmes might be one way of doing this

Patients could be encouraged to attend a patient support group such as Breathe Easy so that the confidence they have gained during the programme is encouraged and maintained. Joining an exercise referral scheme might also help patients maintain their exercise levels following the rehabilitation programme.

## Conclusions

Pulmonary rehabilitation is not currently widely available in the UK, although provision is extending. It has been specifically mentioned in the new NICE/BTS guidelines as being important in the care of the COPD patient. Although the majority of programmes are currently funded, a significant number rely on the good will and enthusiasm of a variety of respiratory-trained health care professionals. At the individual level pulmonary rehabilitation enables patients to adjust to having a chronic condition while encouraging maximum functioning and independence. It is, however, an essentially palliative process in the management of disease, aimed at ameliorating symptoms and assisting individual coping mechanisms. Programmes also appear to be able to reduce the burden of the disease upon the individual, and their family with positive consequences for the NHS.

**Therefore, to summarise the key points:**

■ Pulmonary rehabilitation is a combination of exercise, education and support.

■ Although pulmonary rehabilitation is often offered in the hospital setting the location of the programme is less important than the content.

■ Optimal pharmacological management is necessary prior to patients under-taking rehabilitation.

■ Pulmonary rehabilitation has a significant role to play in the management of COPD and has benefits both for patients and the health economy.

■ Multi-professional working has been found to contribute to the success of pulmonary rehabilitation although success can equally be found in programmes run by one enthusiastic individual

■ Patients are selected for pulmonary rehabilitation on the basis of their own recognition of the degree of disability associated with COPD, currently MRC 3 and above.

A modular diploma programme in pulmonary rehabilitation is available through the Respiratory ETC:

e-mail info@respiratoryetc.com; www.respiratoryetc.com.

---

## What could I do?

■ Ensure patients have access to pulmonary rehabilitation.

■ Lobby for funding if necessary.

■ Consider primary care as an appropriate care setting.

■ Acknowledge the benefit of input from different health care professionals.

# Further reading

ACCP/AACVPR Pulmonary Rehabilitation Guidelines Panel (1997) Pulmonary rehabilitation. Joint ACCP/AACVPR Evidence based guidelines. *Chest,* **112**:1363–1396.

American Thoracic Society (1999) Pulmonary rehabilitation. *Am. J. Respir. Crit. Care Med.,* **159**: No. 5, 1666–1682.

Bestall, J.C., Paul, E.A., Garrod, R., Garnham, R., Jones, P.W., Wedzicha, J.A., *et al* (1999) Usefulness of the Medical Research Council (MRC) dyspnoea scale as a measure of disability in patients with chronic obstructive pulmonary disease. *Thorax,* **54**:581–586.

British Thoracic Society Standards of Care Subcommittee on Pulmonary Rehabilitation (2001) Pulmonary rehabilitation. Standards of care. *Thorax,* **56**:827–834.

Green, R.H., Singh, S.J., Williams, J. and Morgan, M.D.L. (2001) A randomised controlled trial of four weeks versus seven weeks of pulmonary rehabilitation in chronic obstructive pulmonary disease. *Thorax,* **56**:143–145.

Griffiths, T.L., Burr, M.L., Campbell, I.A., Lewis-Jenkins, V., Mullins, J., Shiels, K., *et al* (2000) Results at 1 year of outpatient multidisciplinary pulmonary rehabilitation: a randomised controlled trial. *Lancet,* **355**:362–368.

Griffiths, T.L., Phillips, C.J., Davies, S., Burr, M.L. and Campbell, I.A. (2001) Cost effectiveness of an outpatient multidisciplinary pulmonary rehabilitation programme. *Thorax,* **56**:779–784.

Guyatt, G.H., Berman, L.B., Townsend, M., Pugsley, S.O. and Chambers, L.W. (1987) A measure of quality of life for clinical trials in chronic lung disease. *Thorax,* **42**:773–778.

Horowitz, M.B., Littenberg, B. and Maher, D.A. (1996) Dyspnoea ratings for prescribing exercise intensity in patients with COPD. *Chest,* **109**:1169–1175.

Jones, P.W., Quirk, F.H., Baveystock, C.M. and Littlejohns, P. (1992) A self complete measure for chronic airflow limitation – the St George's Respiratory Questionnaire. *Am. Rev. Respir. Dis.,* **145**:1321–1327.

Kaplan, R.M., Eakin, E.G. and Ries, A.L. (1993) Psychosocial issues in the rehabiliation of patients with COPD. In Casaburi and Petty (eds) *Principles and Practices of Pulmonary Rehabilitation.* WB Saunders Company.

Lacasse, Y., Wong, E., Guyatt, G.H., King, D., Cook, D.J. and Goldstein, R.S. (1996) Meta analysis of respiratory rehabilitation in chronic obstructive pulmonary disease. *Lancet,* **348**:1115–1119.

Landbo, C., Prescott, E., Lange, P., Vestbo, J. and Almdal, T.P. (1999) Prognostic value of nutritional status in chronic obstructive pulmonary disease. *Am. J. Respir. Crit. Care Med.,* **160**:1856–1861.

Law, M., Baptiste, S., McColl, M.A., et al (1994) *The Canadian Occupational Performance Measure, 2nd Edition.* CAOT Publications, Toronto.

Mason, L., Singh, S.J. and Morgan, M.D.L. (1999) Improvements in domestic function after pulmonary rehabilitation. *Thorax,* **54**(suppl 3): A17.

Morgan, M. and Singh, S. (1997) *Practical Pulmonary Rehabilitation.* Chapman and Hall Medical.

National Institutes of Health, National Heart, Lung and Blood Institute (2001) Global strategy for the diagnosis, management and prevention of chronic obstructive disease. 2701. NIH, Bethesda, MD (also available online at www.goldcopd.com).

Singh, S.J., Morgan, M.D.L., Harman, A.E., et al (1992) Development of a shuttle walking test of disability in patients with chronic airways obstruction. *Thorax,* **47**:1019–1024.

Troosters, T., Gosselink, R. and Decramer, M. (2000) Short- and long-term effects of outpatient rehabilitation in patients with chronic obstructive pulmonary disease: a randomized trial. *Am. J. Med.,* **109**: 207–212.

Turner, A. (1997) Foundations for practice in occupational therapy and physical dysfunction. In Turner, A., Foster. M & Johnson, S.E. (eds) *Occupational Therapy and Physical Dysfunction. Principles, Skills and Practice.* Churchill Livingstone, New York.

Ware, J.E. (1994) The status of health assessment. *Ann. Rev. Pub. Health.,* **16**:327–354.

Zigmond, A.S. and Snaith, R.P. (1983) The Hospital Anxiety and Depression Scale. *Acta Psychiatr. Scand.,* **67**:361–370.

# Chapter **11**

## Domiciliary Oxygen for those with COPD

**In this chapter:**

Anyone who is hypoxaemic, for whatever reason, can benefit from supplementary oxygen therapy.

Long-term oxygen therapy (LTOT) prolongs survival in those with COPD.

The key criteria for prescribing LTOT in COPD are described.

The indication for overnight sleep studies is outlined.

Methods of providing and administering supplementary oxygen are set out.

The use of ambulatory oxygen is discussed.

The cost of domiciliary oxygen services in England alone has increased from just over £30 million per year in 1996 to over £42 million in the year 2002. Nearly a third more is spent on the provision of oxygen cylinders than is spent on the provision of oxygen concentrators. At present, hospital services arrange the investigations to determine who needs supplementary oxygen, and primary care physicians then write the prescriptions and community pharmacists supply cylinder oxygen or contractors supply oxygen concentrators. In the UK, from 2005, responsibility for prescription and assessment will move from primary care to hospital specialists as happens now in Scotland, and local contractors will work with local chest physicians and patients to determine how best to fill the prescription. General practitioners will continue to prescribe oxygen for patients who need small quantities. However, all who care for those with respiratory illness will still need to know which patients require assessment of their need for additional oxygen.

## Who needs oxygen at home?

The short answer to this is anybody who is hypoxaemic. However we need to recognise that, hypothetically, hypoxia could result from any of the following pathophysiological processes:

- ventilation perfusion mismatching

- hypoventilation

- diffusion impairment

- shunt

- high altitude.

In practice most people with lung disease are hypoxic because of ventilation perfusion mismatching or hypoventilation. It is vital that treatment of the underlying condition is optimised before the necessity or otherwise for supplementary oxygen is considered.

While this book is concerned with COPD, we should recognise that others could need to be considered for long-term oxygen. These include:

- those with heart disease (congenital heart disease, congestive cardiac failure)

- those with neuromuscular disorders (often in conjunction with ventilatory support)

- children (premature newborns, post-ventilatory sequelae/early life insults).

Patients with the following lung diseases might also need to be considered for supplementary oxygen at home:

- COPD

- cystic fibrosis

- primary and secondary pulmonary malignancies

- asbestosis

- fibrosing alveolitis

- scoliosis/post-thoracoplasty

- pulmonary vascular disorders.

## When do people with lung disease need to be considered for supplementary oxygen therapy?

Consideration for supplementary oxygen is necessary when a patient's arterial blood oxygen tension is below 8 kPa, because pulmonary heart disease and renal hypoxia and dependent oedema then become increasingly common. Once these adverse features are present, the 5-year survival for COPD, for example, could be less than 50%.

## What is the evidence that long-term oxygen therapy (LTOT) prolongs survival in those with COPD?

The UK Medical Research Council Long Term Domiciliary Oxygen Therapy Working Party published the results of its trial in *The Lancet* in 1981. In this study, patients were randomised to receive either usual care or supplementary oxygen for at least 15 h daily. A total of 19 of the 42 patients treated with oxygen (45%) died during the 5 years of follow-up compared with 30 out of 45 (67%) in the control group. It was difficult to predict from these patients which adverse features pointed to a likely poor outcome, but the numerical summation of $CO_2$ level and red cell mass was a pointer to an adverse outcome. Interestingly in the male patients the advantages of LTOT only became apparent 500 days after admission to the trial, but an earlier benefit was apparent from the females in the trial, but there were smaller numbers and this data must not be over-interpreted. The MRC study thus suggested that 15 h of supplementary oxygen per day was beneficial. Around the same time, the US National Heart, Lung & Blood Institute Nocturnal Oxygen Therapy Treatment Study was reported in the *Annals of Internal Medicine*. This study had no control arm but it compared 12 h of oxygen per day (102 patients) with 24 h of oxygen per day (101 patients). Results showed that the mean annual death rate was reduced very significantly in those breathing oxygen for the longer time period (i.e. most of the time).

The MRC study did not show any beneficial reduction of rates of hospitalisation but the numbers in the study were relatively small. A subsequent Danish study reported in 2002 by Ringbaek *et al.* in the *European Respiratory Journal* looked at 246 patients with COPD and showed an overall 23.8% reduction in hospitalisation rates after patients were started on LTOT compared with a pre-treatment period. There was also a significant reduction in the number of hospital days used. The patients' compliance with oxygen therapy influenced the outcomes, in that those that breathed oxygen for between 15 and 24 h a day had better outcomes than those breathing < 15 h of oxygen a day, where the beneficial effect on reducing hospitalisation rates was less apparent.

## What are the criteria for LTOT for COPD?

The key criteria for prescribing LTOT for COPD are:

- $PaO_2$ < 7.3 kPa when stable breathing air for at least 30 min after last breathing supplementary oxygen, or

- $PaO_2$ between 7.3 and 8 when stable, but with one of the following:

  - secondary polycythaemia

  - nocturnal hypoxemia ($SaO_2$ < 90% for more than 30% of the time)

  - peripheral oedema or pulmonary hypertension.

It is very important to note that these criteria must be fulfilled when the patient is in a **stable** condition, and that arterial blood-gas estimations to assess eligibility for oxygen therapy should be repeated at least 4 weeks apart. It should be noted that up to 40% of patients who are thought to be eligible for LTOT at the time of an exacerbation would no longer fulfil the criteria when blood-gas estimation is repeated 3 weeks later. It is therefore important for hospitals to have systems in place such that the patient being discharged from hospital after an admission for an exacerbation of COPD can have their blood gases estimated in a medical assessment or medical day unit a month or so after discharge. Such a unit is an appropriate place for primary care to be able to refer such patients for the serial blood-gas monitoring that is necessary for the adequate evaluation of patients' oxygen needs. Ideally each hospital should provide an oxygen assessment clinic where evaluation is undertaken according to set protocols and where clinical scientists, occupational therapists and respiratory nurse specialists were in attendance.

## Are sleep studies necessary in these patients?

Oxygen levels during the day usually mirror those at night. However, some patients do require overnight sleep studies and these are indicated when any of the following are present:

- oxygen levels seem very low for the degree of reduction in $FEV_1$

- oedema persists despite correction of daytime hypoxaemia

- patients complain of disorientation on waking or morning headaches (a feature of nocturnal $CO_2$ retention)

- there are any features (such as snoring, obesity, excessive daytime sleepiness) to suggest associated obstructive sleep apnoea syndrome

- there are associated skeletal or neuromuscular abnormalities.

## Do the same indications for LTOT apply to diseases other than COPD?

Most of the studies of LTOT have been performed on patients with COPD. However, it seems reasonable to consider this therapy in the same way for patients with diffuse parenchymal lung diseases, including fibrosing alveolitis, sarcoidosis and asbestosis and for patients with end-stage respiratory failure (for example, secondary to cystic fibrosis).

## How can LTOT be provided?

The possible methods of providing LTOT are outlined below.

### Cylinders

For those requiring to breathe oxygen for more than 15 h a day, this is not a practical possibility as it is very difficult to deliver the number of cylinders required on a regular basis to the home.

## Oxygen concentrators

These currently represent the most common method of providing home oxygen for long-term use *(see Fig. 27)*. A molecular sieve removes nitrogen from room air, giving 95% oxygen. The concentration falls at higher flow-rates, and this has relevance to the way in which we assess patients' needs. When determining the flow-rate a patient needs to correct their hypoxemia to a waking $PaO_2 > 8$ kPa this should be estimated with the patient breathing oxygen from the type of concentrator they are likely to use at home and not, for example, by breathing 100% oxygen from a cylinder or from a piped hospital oxygen supply.

**Figure 27.** An oxygen concentrator. Such machines from a variety of contractors can be installed in patients' homes and their electrical running costs reimbursed. Siting within the home requires care to reduce any nuisance from noise, and outlet taps need to be placed near to the favourite sitting room chair and in the bedroom *(Illustration supplied by Air Products plc.)*

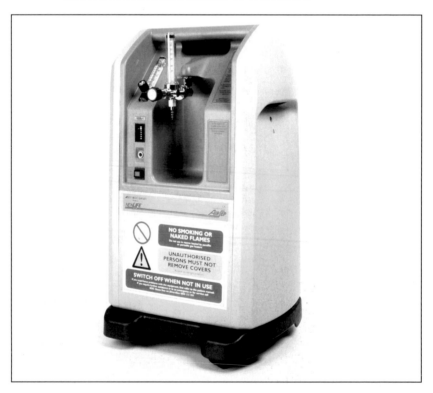

It is very important that care and consideration is given to the placement of such a concentrator within the home, as these machines can be noisy and can also concentrate other gases. They should not, for example, be placed under a stairwell next to a gas meter. One study by Dilworth *et al.* in 1990 of 30 patients on LTOT, showed that only 34% of patients had more than one outlet from their oxygen concentrator, and that this makes it harder for them to use oxygen in the bedroom, bathroom, or on the stairs, as well as in the main living room. A total of 70% of patients in that study had a concentrator placed in their main room, where it was a potential source of noise pollution.

**Figure 28.** Liquid oxygen is widely used in the USA and in Scotland and will be more widely available in the UK after 2005. For those on LTOT and supplementary ambulatory oxygen the same source can be used for fully portable devices for supplementary ambulatory oxygen and used for long-term oxygen supplementation *(Illustration supplied by Air Products plc.)*

## Liquid oxygen

This can be provided in 30–50 litre oxygen tanks. This method is commonly used in the USA and is available in Scotland *(see Fig. 28)*. It should be available in the rest of the UK under the new oxygen service arrangements from the year 2005 onwards. It has the advantage that it can be used to fill portable tanks, though the oxygen does evaporate from these tanks if not used. Careful instruction is also necessary in order to avoid frostbite or burns from close contact with the tanks. Liquid oxygen can also be more expensive.

## How is the oxygen administered to the patients?

Supplementary oxygen for long-term usage can be used either through a Venturi face-mask or by soft nasal cannulae/prongs. Most patients find the latter preferable because it permits mobility by the use of long lengths of tubing (the weight of which sometimes pulls a mask from the face), and nasal cannulae also make eating and conversation easier.

## What information do patients need?

Patients should be given information *(see Fig. 29)* about their diagnosis and the number of hours that they should breath their oxygen; they also clearly need advice regarding back-up, servicing and follow-up arrangements. Some might require information about the availability of humidifiers, and of course all patients need advice regarding the dangers of smoking. Patients might also need advice regarding travel, portable concentrators and the use of other forms of ambulatory oxygen outside the home.

## What follow-up of patients on LTOT is necessary?

All patients should be followed-up in their own home by a respiratory health care professional who will check the adequacy of the supplementary oxygen by measurement of oxygen saturation, and will reinforce advice regarding the hours of use and the dangers of smoking, etc. All patients also need to be followed-up by a hospital specialist to maintain optimisation of their other therapies and to watch for signs of cardiac decompensation, oedema or sleep-related worsening. All patients need to be reassessed with repeat arterial blood-gas estimations at approximately yearly intervals.

**Figure 29.** An example of a written leaflet used to provide patients with COPD with information regarding LTOT. Patients with COPD need to be given clear advice about their diagnosis, their treatment, the number of hours during which they should breathe supplementary oxygen and advice regarding humidifiers, back-up oxygen cylinders and reimbursement of electricity costs

The Hammersmith Hospitals **NHS**
NHS Trust

Charing Cross Hospital
Fulham Palace Rd.
LONDON
W6 8RF

# HOME OXYGEN

Everything y₀
know about a
concent

## Will I be housebound?

No! Many people who need oxygen constantly are given portable oxygen. See leaflet on 'ambulatory oxygen' for details.

## Do's and Don'ts

- Don't smoke while using oxygen and warn visitors not to smoke near you when you are using oxygen. Put up no-smoking signs in your home where you most often use the oxygen.

- **Oxygen is explosive**. Stay at least five feet away from gas stoves, candles, lighted fireplaces, or other heat sources.

- Don't use any flammable products like cleaning fluid, paint thinner, or aerosol sprays while using your oxygen.

- Notify your electric company so you will be given priority if there is a power failure.

- Use water-based lubricants on your lips or nostrils. Don't use an oil-based product like petroleum jelly (Vaseline)

- To stop your cheeks or the skin behind your ears getting irritated, tuck something soft under the tubing.

## Who needs ambulatory oxygen?

Patients who should be considered for ambulatory oxygen are:

- those on LTOT who are able to, and want to, leave the home

- those who have no need for LTOT but who desaturate on exertion and who can exercise more on supplementary oxygen.

The type of ambulatory oxygen provided would depend upon the patients' need, most especially the duration of that need and the flow-rate. It should be recalled that the PD-sized portable oxygen cylinder available on the drug tariff will last for nearly 4 h at a flow-rate of 1 l/min, half that time at 2 l/min, only 1 h at 4 l/min, and only 45 min at 6 l/min. Patients who need to be out of the house for some time, or who have a need for higher flow-rates, will clearly have problems obtaining enough portable oxygen. Because of this, a variety of oxygen-conserving devices have been tried, and these reflect the understanding that more than half of the respiratory cycle is spent on breathing out, and that oxygen flowing during that time is wasted. Some reservoir systems that lie along the upper lip and store the flow of oxygen that occurs during expiration can halve the wastage of oxygen. Other pulse delivery systems that are activated by inspiration deliver a bolus of oxygen within the first 200 ms of inspiration, and these can prolong cylinder usage by up to 4-times. These are not currently available on the drug tariff, but can be obtained by some chest departments and will hopefully be available under the new regulations.

## How do we assess whether somebody would benefit from ambulatory oxygen?

It is very important to realise that with ambulatory oxygen the energy cost of transporting the oxygen, whether by carrying it or by pushing it on a trolley, needs to be incorporated into the assessment. Some physicians adopt an empirical attitude that if patients feel better on supplementary oxygen during exercise, they should be provided with it. This practice should be discouraged, and proper assessment via a walking test is the preferred approach; either the standard 6 min walking test or the shuttle walking test can be utilised *(see pg 115 and Fig. 30)*. After a practice, the patient undergoes one or other of these tests in random order, breathing either air from a cylinder or oxygen from a cylinder; the cylinders should be covered so that the patient is unaware which gas they are breathing. The patient should be assessed with oxygen saturation monitoring during this exercise so that the degree of desaturation can be determined. They should also be asked to score subjectively how they felt on both exercises using either a simple visual analogue scale or the BORG Perception of Dyspnoea Scale. Most authorities would regard an improvement of 10% or more in the walking distance or the dyspnoea score on oxygen as being ample justification for a supply of ambulatory oxygen.

**Figure 30.** Results of a Shuttle Walk Test performed on air and oxygen in a 45-year-old woman with severe COPD secondary to α1-antitrypsin deficiency. Exercise capacity subsequently improved significantly during the breathing of supplementary oxygen

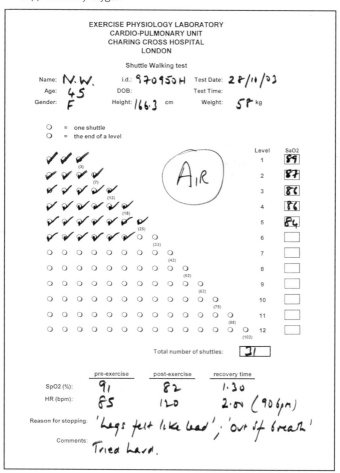

## Conclusions

Availability of oxygen of different types and service provision for assessment varies in different parts of the country, but the most important aspect is to recognise that the patient might benefit from supplementary oxygen and to refer them for appropriate assessment to a local centre.

## What could I do?

■ Ensure patients with severe COPD are assessed for LTOT and for ambulatory oxygen.

■ Reinforce to patients how to use their supplementary oxygen to maximum effect.

■ Remind patients of the importance of not smoking, especially in the presence of the oxygen supplier.

■ Maximise non-oxygen therapies and ensure regular review.

## Further reading

Dilworth, J.P., Higgs, C.M.B., Jones, P.A. and White, R.J. (1990) Acceptability of oxygen concentrators: the patient's view. *Br. J. Gen. Pract.*, **40**:415–417.

Medical Research Council (1981) Long term domiciliary oxygen therapy in chronic hypoxic cor pulmonale complicating chronic bronchitis and emphysema. Report of a working party. *Lancet*, **1**:681–686.

Nocturnal Oxygen Therapy Trial Group (1980) Continuous or nocturnal oxygen therapy in hypoxemic chronic obstructive lung disease: A clinical trial. *Ann. Intern. Med.*, **93**:391–398.

Ringbaek, T.J., Viskum, K. and Lange, P. (2002) Does long-term oxygen therapy reduce hospitalisation in hypoxaemic chronic obstructive pulmonary disease? *Eur. Respir. J.*, **20**:38–42.

# Chapter 12

# Investigation of COPD in Secondary Care and Rarer Differential Diagnosis

**In this chapter:**

The features that characterise emphysema are detailed.

Significant co-morbidity, particularly severe heart failure and interstitial lung diseases have an effect on spirometry and other measures of lung function.

In patients with COPD and co-existent cardiac disease, it is now possible through sophisticated combined cardiopulmonary exercise tests (CPET) to identify which of the two conditions is exercise-limiting.

The value of High Resolution CT (HRCT) scanning of the chest is described.

Co-existent systemic features in a relatively young person with respiratory symptoms should raise the suspicion of a multi-system disease.

Diagnosis of COPD is, in the vast majority of cases, a relatively uncomplicated exercise. However, when the common respiratory symptoms that raise the suspicion of COPD (breathlessness and cough) are either solely, or partly, due to other chronic cardiorespiratory conditions, including heart disease, difficulties can be encountered in making the diagnosis. This chapter discusses briefly the more specialist investigations that are often deployed in secondary care to investigate possible COPD.

## Lung function tests in secondary care

Spirometry on its own enables the diagnosis of COPD to be made in the vast majority of cases. However, in secondary care, a systematic combination of lung function tests are carried out and a more detailed analysis of the patterns of abnormalities from these lung function tests is used to delineate more clearly the presence of emphysematous COPD. The two tests of lung function that are often carried out routinely as part of 'full lung function testing', in addition to spirometry, are the measurement of lung volumes and diffusing capacity.

## Lung volume measurements

These are made by getting the patient to breathe, through a closed system, a known concentration of helium from a known volume of gas. After the gas has been allowed to equilibrate fully with the patients' lungs, the concentration of helium in measured again and the volume of the lungs estimated by the application of Boyle's law. Helium dilution thus allows the measurement of total lung capacity (TLC) and its various components including residual volume (RV), which is the amount of air that is left behind in the lung after a maximal expiration. Typically, in patients with airflow obstruction the lungs are of increased volume, thereby elevating the TLC, and show some features of air trapping or hyperinflation with the proportion of residual volume to total lung capacity (RV/TLC) being higher than average. Emphysema is thus typified by an elevated TLC and a high RV/TLC ratio.

## Diffusing capacity measurements

These are carried out by estimating the uptake of CO (carbon monoxide) by the pulmonary gas exchange mechanism. Gas exchange across the lungs, i.e. movement of oxygen in and $CO_2$ out, is dependent on the integrity of both the alveolar membrane and the pulmonary circulation; abnormalities of either can disrupt this process. In emphysema, which is characterised by the destruction of the alveolar membrane, this capacity for gas exchange is compromised and the low diffusing capacity that can occur in moderate to severe emphysema is often a good predictor of the systemic effects of COPD, including poor exercise capacity and weight loss. It is worth highlighting that measurement of diffusing capacity requires the subject to hold their breath for a 10-second period, and those patients who are very breathless at rest and those with very poor lung function might not be able to perform this test.

## Interpretation of lung function tests in the presence of co-morbidity

A significant proportion of elderly patients with COPD suffer cardiac co-morbidity. The stiff, oedematous lungs in patients with significant pulmonary congestion can cause a 'restrictive' lung defect, and during spirometry this can render the obstructive defect from COPD less strikingly evident. The obstructive picture of a reduced $FEV_1/FVC$ ratio can be accompanied by a co-existent absolute reduction in both these values, making for a combined obstructive and restrictive defect. A similar situation pertains in patients with co-existent 'restrictive' disorders such as interstitial lung disease, thoracic cage deformities (scoliosis) and morbid obesity, which reduce both $FEV_1$ and FVC. In these circumstances imaging techniques, including high resolution CT scanning of the lungs, may be of much value.

## Advanced imaging in COPD

Although COPD is not a radiological diagnosis, it is not uncommon for chest X-rays requested from primary care to be reported as showing COPD. Hyperinflation, as revealed by flattened diaphragmatic shadows and large lungs, an increased volume of retrosternal air space on lateral films, a narrow cardiac silhouette and general hypertransluceny of the lung fields are the features that usually prompt such a diagnosis. However, these changes caused by emphysema are evident only in the more advanced stages of the disease when lung function is unequivocally compromised. Over the past decade the advent of high resolution CT (HRCT) scanning has revolutionised the imaging of the lungs, and it is now evident that HRCT is a very sensitive and specific tool in the diagnosis of emphysema. Also, the ability of HRCT scans of the lung to reveal marked abnormalities in the lung fields in patients with interstitial lung disease (fibrosing alveolitis, sarcoidosis, asbestosis, etc.) in the presence of an apparently 'normal' chest X-ray is now well recognised, so much so that HRCT is now a mandatory investigation in the diagnosis of interstitial lung disease.

Given these developments, although HRCT scanning of the chest is not a routine investigation in the diagnosis of emphysema and COPD, it is a very valuable diagnostic aid in the management of patients who suffer from more than one lung disease and, in particular, those with COPD and a co-existent fibrotic or other interstitial lung disease.

HRCT also aids the identification of bullae and the delineation of the anatomical distribution of the emphysematous abnormalities. This information is valuable in assessing the feasibility, scope and potential benefit from surgical treatments

**Table 24.** CT scanning in COPD

---

High resolution CT (HRCT) scanning of the chest is not routinely recommended in the investigation of COPD; the investigation, however, has a very high sensitivity and specificity in diagnosing emphysema.

HRCT scans are particularly valuable in demonstrating the presence and extent of bullae; the test also helps in assessing the anatomical distribution of emphysema, aiding in decision making as regards surgery (bullectomy; lung volume reduction surgery) as a treatment.

HRCT scans are crucial to the diagnosis of interstitial lung diseases (fibrosing alveolitis, sarcoidosis, asbestosis, etc.) and are now a mandatory investigation in the diagnosis and management of these conditions.

CT scans have replaced bronchograms as the investigation of choice in bronchiectasis.

Whereas CT scans of the chest performed in COPD patients for other reasons may occasionally show up a solitary pulmonary nodule or features of early lung cancer, it is not recommended that CT scans of the chest are performed as a screening test for lung cancer in COPD patients.

such as bullectomy and lung volume reduction surgery. It should be borne in mind that patients with COPD are at high risk of lung cancer and CT scans of the chest performed for other reasons can occasionally show up a solitary pulmonary nodule or other abnormality suggestive of early lung cancer. However, routine surveillance CT scanning of COPD patients to detect early lung cancer is not currently recommended.

The other condition where CT scans of the chest have made a critical difference is in the diagnosis of bronchiectasis. HRCT scans are able to detect even minor degrees of dilatation of the airways and are now the investigation of choice in diagnosing bronchiectasis, rendering obsolete the traditional investigation of bronchography.

*Table 24* shows a summary of the usefulness of CT scanning in COPD.

## Rarer differential diagnosis of COPD and some pointers to their identification in primary care

In previous chapters we have dealt with the more common differential diagnoses of COPD. In most instances a good history and physical examination will enable the distinction of COPD from the conditions listed. Very occasionally, rare illnesses including interstitial lung diseases and other obstructive lung diseases such as obiliterative bronchiolitis can present with symptoms and signs that can be difficult to differentiate from COPD or, even more tryingly, occur in combination with COPD, rendering initial diagnosis extremely difficult.

*Table 25* shows some of the other conditions that might be eventually diagnosed in secondary care with the aid of specialist investigations, but can present with symptoms akin to COPD in primary care. In general, systemic symptoms, particularly relating to joints, skin (rash), mucous membranes (ulcers) and eyes, occurring in a relatively young person or in the absence of a very strong smoking history should raise the suspicion of a multi-system disease such as rheumatoid arthritis or systemic lupus erythematosus (SLE). In these patients urinalysis (dipstick testing) to detect proteinuria or haematuria (as a manifestation of renal involvement) is a useful test that can be performed in the setting of primary care. The primary care physician might also consider requesting an auto-antibody screen (rheumatoid factor; anti-nuclear antibody and antibody to double-stranded DNA in SLE) while the referral to secondary care is being made in consideration of these diagnoses.

**Table 25.** Rarer differential diagnoses of COPD

**Pulmonary fibrosis/fibrosing alveolitis**
(either alone or associated with rheumatoid arthritis, SLE, scleroderma)
Cough (often dry) and progressive dyspnoea over months or years; systemic (joints, skin, eye) symptoms and signs; clubbing (in about 50%) and crackles on auscultation of the lung fields; restrictive abnormality on lung function testing; typical imaging abnormalities on HRCT scanning of the chest

**Sarcoidosis**
Afro-Caribbean origin (can affect all ethnic groups, however); previous erythema nodosum; joint eye or other systemic features; elevated ACE (angiotensin-converting enzyme) levels in blood (NB Kviem test is no longer performed); restrictive abnormality on lung function testing; characteristic abnormalities on imaging by chest X ray or CT scan (interstitial shadowing; hilar adenopathy)

**Obiliterative bronchiolitis**
Severe airflow obstruction with no reversibility in the context of conditions such as rheumatoid arthritis or post-lung transplant; no evidence of emphysema on imaging; CT scanning is very helpful in distinguishing severe irreversible airflow obstruction caused by emphysema and obiliterative bronchiolitis; poor prognosis with life expectancy from time of diagnosis at less than 3 years

**Extrinsic allergic alveolitis**
Cough and dyspnoea; history of exposure to specific antigens known to cause the condition [pigeons; mouldy hay (farmer's lung) etc.]. Crackles on examination of the chest; characteristic CT scan appearances; often a combination of restrictive and obstructive abnormalities on lung function tests

**Asbestosis**
Exposure to asbestos usually decades previously (building trade, electricians, boilers, work in the power industry); the patients might not have handled asbestos themselves; clubbing; crackles in the chest; restrictive abnormality on lung function tests; HRCT scans could reveal pleural (plaques; diffuse pleural thickening and more rarely mesothelioma) and lung parenchymal pathology

**Progressive massive fibrosis**
In retired coal miners in association with pneumoconiosis; there might be no signs in the chest but radiological appearances are usually characteristic.

## Conclusions

In the vast majority of cases, the diagnosis of COPD can be made on the basis of a good history and spirometry. However, in a few patients – particularly those with cardiorespiratory co-morbidity, including heart disease – achieving a diagnosis may be helped by the performance of more detailed physiological measurements and imaging in secondary care. High resolution CT scanning is particularly valuable in identifying patients with bronchiectasis and interstitial lung disease. In patients presenting with systemic symptoms (particularly younger non-smokers), consideration must be given to a diagnosis of lung disease occurring as part of multi-system disorders such as sarcoidosis and SLE.

## What could I do?

- Refer patients with an unclear history, symptoms, signs or test results for specialist help with diagnosis.

- Be aware of the rare conditions which can present like COPD and may require specialist investigations to diagnose (see also *Chapter 1*).

## Further reading

Diagnosing COPD. In Chronic Obstructive Pulmonary Disease. National Clinical Guideline on management of chronic obstructive pulmonary disease in adults in primary and secondary care (2004) *Thorax*, **59**(suppl 1):27–37.

Van Schayak, C.P., Loozen, J.M., Wagena, E., Akkermans, R.P. and Wesseling, G.J. (2002) Detecting patients at a high risk of developing chronic obstructive pulmonary disease in general practice: cross sectional case finding study. *BMJ*, **324**:1370–1374.

# Chapter **13**

## Providing an Integrated
## Care Service
## for COPD

**In this chapter:**

Existing services can fail to provide a comprehensive and integrated package of care for patients with COPD.

Early diagnosis, smoking cessation support and optimal drug therapy should be offered.

The management of acute exacerbations, both admission where necessary and discharge, must be coordinated.

Pulmonary rehabilitation and palliative care involve may involve different clinicians and agencies.

Intermediate care is an innovative and promising concept.

COPD is a preventable, progressive disease causing increasing symptoms and disability. There are useful treatments for most patients at all stages, but some patients are, unfortunately, still being told 'there is nothing that can be done for you'. As is often the case, a methodical, team approach to managing a patient can provide the best outcomes.

An effective service should incorporate the following features:

- early, accurate diagnosis (using spirometry), supported by hospital investigations where needed

- a smoking cessation service (to limit disease progression)

- pharmacotherapy (to achieve maximal bronchodilatation, symptom control, increase in activities of daily living, exacerbation reduction and associated, non-pulmonary conditions)

- pulmonary rehabilitation and other non-drug treatments (exercise, nutrition, education, motivation and support)

- early intervention in exacerbations with antibiotics/steroids

- in-patient facilities for the acutely ill

- referral for long-term oxygen assessment for all suitable patients

- psychosocial support for severely ill patients

- palliative care.

It is important to identify and register patients on databases at various stages of their disease and health care pathway to promote annual review and ensure that they are referred to appropriate services. It is commonplace to find that those with early disease are not offered a comprehensive smoking cessation package. Additionally, pulmonary rehabilitation programmes may have vacancies while distressed patients, in need of rehabilitation, are not being referred. Good communication between the primary, intermediate and secondary care staff is essential.

## Primary care and spirometry

In the UK about two-thirds of practices own a spirometer. To ensure their appropriate use, spirometers should only be used by staff who have undergone proper training, with supervised assessment of their skills. Training needs to be updated periodically.

To maintain the user's skills, spirometry should be performed frequently, and support is needed when there is doubt about results and how to interpret them.

Spirometry can be performed on asymptomatic smokers, those with smoker's cough, dyspnoea or acute bronchitis. Realistically, identification of COPD in its early stages can only be done in primary care.

Performing spirometry reliably and consistently in primary care is not without difficulties. This has been recognised by primary care organisations and various models of providing support to primary care have been proposed *(see Table 26)*. One system incorporates accurate spirometry by a visiting expert (it is not important from which discipline they come). They, with support from specialists, make a formal diagnosis and leave the ongoing care to the primary health care team, who also receive education and support in the care of patients with COPD. Protocols for management and referral are helpful, especially if drawn up locally with involvement and ownership in primary care. Quality standards should be audited including outcomes on smoking cessation. Under the new UK General Medical Services contract, money is paid to practices who achieve quality markers for COPD care *(see Chapter 15)*.

**Table 26.** Options for spirometry

| In-house spirometry | Feedback options |
| --- | --- |
| • Mobile spirometry service visiting practices or operating in community clinics using expert practice nurse, respiratory special nurses or technicians | • Spirometry results |
| | • Interpretation, e.g. obstructive |
| | • Reversibility testing results and interpretation |
| • Hospital-based open access clinics | |
| • Pharmacy-based spirometry service | • Suggestions for therapy |
| | • Suggestions for referral |

## Integrated care for patients with established COPD

Integrated care involves a flexible multi-disciplinary service to encompass all aspects of the disease. Central to the concept is an intermediate care team. The team usually includes respiratory specialist nurses and physiotherapists, with additional support from a GP with a special interest in COPD. The service needs contact with consultants, ward and outpatient staff, the patient's usual primary care staff and managers. Investing in such systems appears to be cost-effective as they save money on hospital admissions and other health and social care costs.

## Exacerbations

Much of the morbidity and health service costs of COPD relate to unscheduled care. Many hospital admissions can be avoided and early discharge schemes are cost-effective and popular with patients. This usually involves an acute assessment and intervention service, delivered at home by specialist nurses, working to protocols. This will include pulse oximetry and spirometry. If hospital assessment is needed, e.g. for chest X-ray or blood gases, or admission is necessary, the process is facilitated, together with early supported discharge to home, nursing home or community hospital. If admission is not necessary, a comprehensive package of care, often called the 'hospital-at-home' scheme can be provided.

These services can be coordinated by a respiratory specialist nurse. The nurse may also be involved in education and rehabilitation and linking with social services. Less severe exacerbations, or those in patients with milder disease, can often be self-managed by patients themselves *(see Chapter 9)* providing they have:

- education about self management

- appropriate contact phone numbers for emergencies

- support from appropriate staff (nurses / physiotherapists) when required

- Social service support for themselves and their carers.

### Pulmonary rehabilitation

Pulmonary rehabilitation programmes are effective at improving exercise tolerance and quality of life *(see Chapter 10)*. They are increasingly becoming part of integrated care services for COPD, often in community settings. An integrated care service incorporates pulmonary rehabilitation for all patients with moderate to severe disease, especially if they are at risk of admissions for exacerbations.

## Putting it all together: an integrated care service

There are various models of integrated care, but central to most are respiratory specialist nurses. In the model shown below *(Fig. 31)*, they work with physiotherapists and a GP with special interest. The whole service is organised by a COPD pathways group, which involves consultants, ward and outpatient staff and managers. Written pathways for management can be an effective way of optimising care and improving communication between hospital and the community.

## Conclusions

COPD is a chronic, progressive, debilitating disease where breathlessness dominates patients' lives. In severe COPD, quality of life is very poor, indeed often worse than in those dying of lung cancer. These patients have been neglected in the past, and new services are needed to provide for the psychological, social and medical needs of both patient and their carer. An integrated care service can provide a complete package from early diagnosis to palliative care. Such services are usually cost-effective. Failure to provide them leads to unnecessary use of expensive treatments and hospital care. COPD is one of many chronic diseases that requires a coordinated approach between primary and secondary care and the development of intermediate care facilities, such as respiratory specialist nurses and pulmonary rehabilitation in the community.

---

## What could I do?

■ Promote delivery of, or access to, all components of an effective COPD service.

■ Support team working.

■ Facilitate communication between primary and secondary care, between health care disciplines and with carers.

**Figure 31.** Model of an integrated care system

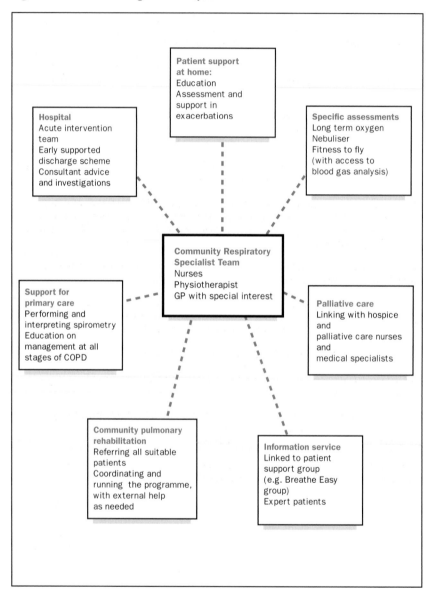

## Further reading

Bridging the Gap, The Respiratory Alliance (2003)
http://www.gpiag-asthma.org/documents/bridging_gap.htm.

Crockett, A.J., Cranston, J.M., Moss, J.R. and Alpers, J.H. (2002) The impact of anxiety, depression and living alone in chronic obstructive pulmonary disease. *Qual. Life Res.,* **11**:309–316.

Gravil, J.H., Al Rawas, O.A., Cotton, M.M., Flanigan, U., Irwin, A. and Stevenson, R.D. (1998) Home treatment of exacerbations of chronic obstructive pulmonary disease by an acute respiratory assessment service. *Lancet,* **351**:1853–1855.

Managing passengers with respiratory disease planning air travel: British Thoracic Society recommendations 218 (2002). *Thorax,* **57**:289–304.

Monninkhof, E.M., van der Valk, P.D.L.P.M., van der Palen, J., Van Herwaarden, C.L.A., Partridge, M.R. and Zielhuis, G.A. (2003) Self-management education for patients with chronic obstructive pulmonary disease (Cochrane review). *The Cochrane Library, Issue 3.* Oxford: Update Software.

National Primary Care Trust Development Team Information Site On Practitioners With Special Interests: www.natpact.nhs.uk/cms/165.php.

Olseni, L., Midgren, B., Hornblad, Y. and Wollmer, P. (1994) Chest physiotherapy in chronic obstructive pulmonary disease: Forced expiratory technique combined with either postural drainage or positive expiratory pressure breathing. *Respir. Med.,* **88**:435–440.

Rose, C., Wallace, L., Dickson, R., Ayres, J., Lehman, R., Searle, Y., *et al.* (2002) The most effective psychologically-based treatments to reduce anxiety and panic in patients with chronic obstructive pulmonary disease (COPD): A systematic review. *Patient Educ. Couns.,* **47**:311–318.

Smith, B., Appleton, S., Adams, R., Southcott, A., Ruffin, R. (2003) Home care by outreach nursing for chronic obstructive pulmonary disease (Cochrane Review). *The Cochrane Library, Issue 3.* Oxford: Update Software.

Stuart, M. and Weinrich, M. (2004) Integrated health system for chronic disease management: lessons learned from France [Review]. *Chest,* **125**:695–703.

# Chapter 14

## Palliative Care
## in COPD

**In this chapter:**

At least as many patients have severe COPD as have lung cancer.

People with COPD often have worse health status than those with lung cancer.

Palliative care budgets tend to be directed to patients with cancer.

Predicting the time of death from COPD is difficult.

Many needs are social, psychological or spiritual.

Dyspnoea is often the over-riding medical symptom.

Most patients will die during an exacerbation of their condition.

Providing a multidisciplinary approach to the patient and his family.

Historically, palliative care provision has been the preserve for those patients with cancer. The NHS is providing increasing resources for palliative care, but the majority remains within the cancer services. UK National Service Frameworks confirm that end-of-life decisions and terminal care need to be addressed for many conditions, not just cancer. Similar numbers of patients die of COPD and lung cancer, but patients with COPD experience worse health status and receive less supportive care than those with lung cancer. Health care provision needs to address the issue of how best to deliver palliative care to all patients with life limiting disease irrespective of diagnosis.

## What is palliative care?

Palliative care, and in particular the hospice movement, began in the 1960s with the founding of St Christopher's Hospice mainly in response to the recognition of the suffering of many patients with cancer. The palliative care approach aims to improve quality of life for patients and their families faced with incurable disease by preventing and treating suffering. It is an individualised approach that encompasses physical, psychological, social and spiritual support. Palliation is applicable early in the course of the illness. Dying is seen as a natural process and the aim of palliative care is to neither hasten nor postpone death, but to enable patients to live as comfortably and actively as possible until their death.

## Diagnosing terminal COPD

Patients with advanced COPD have a terminal illness. They often have major unrelenting symptoms and their illness is steadily progressive, although there can be periods of stability interspersed with acute exacerbations. Treatment of COPD can be considered essentially palliative because there is no cure; treatment is aimed at damage limitation and amelioration of symptoms.

Predicting the time of death is more difficult in COPD than cancer. Clearly patients have different trajectories of illness, but there are pointers to poor prognosis. Patients with an $FEV_1$ <40% of predicted or those with *cor pulmonale* have a prognosis comparable to advanced lung cancer. A falling BMI and frequent exacerbations also indicate rapid deterioration. It is estimated that around 50% of patients with COPD will die within 2 years of their first admission for an exacerbation. It can be difficult to predict when patients will actually die of COPD as this often happens as a result of, and during, an exacerbation; those with severely damaged lungs can live for a substantial time if they stay free of exacerbations.

# Symptoms of COPD

Common symptoms experienced by patients with COPD are:

- breathlessness

- cough

- excessive or discoloured sputum production

- fatigue

- pain

- insomnia

- anxiety and depression

- fear and panic

- weight loss/cachexia.

The universal symptom for patients with COPD is chronic breathlessness. Breathlessness gets worse over time and is particularly noticeable, troublesome and frightening during acute exacerbations. Patients fear these attacks and worry that the next one may be their last. They can also worry that they will die struggling for their breath and it is often difficult to reassure them. This is a disastrous complex. Furthermore, the sensation of breathlessness is very likely to provoke marked anxiety, and in terminal COPD this can dominate their lives. Breathlessness is often accompanied by depression, lack of motivation, anger, denial, guilt and isolation, very similar to the grieving process seen in malignant disease. The generally negative feelings that patients, society and health care professionals have towards COPD can aggravate the problem. Patients can feel that they have brought it on themselves by smoking, yet many elderly patients started smoking before the harmful effects were recognised. It is ironic that smokers who have cancer or heart disease get more sympathy, although quality of life is much lower in those dying of COPD compared with lung cancer.

Other symptoms are fatigue, which appears to be universal and occurs because of a combination of factors such as impaired oxygenation, lack of fitness, depression, impaired nutrition and poor sleep. Patients can have a host of other issues adding to their gloom: financial concerns; worries about their partner; and about the impact of their disease on their partner's life.

## Symptom control: some basic principles

To manage symptoms, it is first necessary to look at patients' understanding of their disease, what caused it and what they anticipate can be done about it. Perceptions are important. Assessing how the patient perceives their condition is important; it allows for the assessment of general well-being and also of the effectiveness of any treatments. It is necessary to dig deeper than cough, dyspnoea and lung function: fear of dying, panic attacks and relationship issues could be critical to their well-being.

Providing symptom control requires expertise that is often lacking in traditional health care systems. Support given to patients is usually reactive and aimed at crisis intervention, usually symptom led rather than proactive, and aimed at ongoing support. It is also important to understand the needs and wishes of carers and family.

## Support

Many needs are social rather than palliative. Social isolation is common in COPD, as with many other chronic and progressive diseases. Physical limitations can cause isolation and promoting patient independence is essential.

In-patient care is expensive and can be the result of an unwillingness or inability to cope at home. Hospital admission may therefore be related to perceived diminished quality of life rather than the physiological measures of disease severity. Social stresses, low levels of support and low self-esteem will reduce functional status regardless of disease severity.

## Psychosocial needs

Chronic illness is becoming increasingly recognised as one of the most important issues facing western society. Chronic illness puts demands on patients and families to deal with the social and emotional impact of symptoms, disabilities and impending death, medicines and interactions with medical care. Clearly patients with COPD need ongoing input and support, but this is rarely provided in traditional health care models. A range of intermediate care approaches are being tried, often involving respiratory nurse specialists. Nurse specialists working in the community are ideally placed to help with the wider issues arising in palliative care. They need to link with other disciplines including social services, housing, etc., to provide optimum care.

## What patients want and assessing needs

Patients want:

- information and communication

- accurate diagnosis

- support

- rehabilitation

- symptom control

- coordinated care

- control.

It is clear that many of the problems patients face are remediable. The patient might need assessment for home aids, and an occupational therapy assessment in the patient's own home could allow them to manage their condition without having to consider moving to a bungalow, flat or sheltered housing. Perching stools, helping hands, bath and stair rails or stair lifts might be necessary as patients deteriorate. Social services could provide help such as cleaning and shopping. Panic alarms or mobile phones may help feelings of isolation. Some patients could be in unsuitable accommodation and will need help and support in deciding on alternatives. Any discussion of further care that would entail moving needs to be handled sensitively, as many people are very reluctant to move from their family home, however unsuitable it might be. Clearly reassessment is important as a patient's needs change as their disease progresses.

In-depth discussion with a trusted health care professional is necessary to work out the priorities for action. Usually this does not happen. GPs are often too busy and might lack expertise and confidence; hospital outpatient clinics do not often provide this role, and specialist nurses are not always available.

The main issues that can be important to patients are outlined below.

### Information needs
Information is a high priority for any dying patient – *'I can cope with what I know.'* As many of the concerns are difficult to talk about, it is crucial to have a trusted professional. Special skills are needed and palliative care communications skills training can be beneficial for respiratory specialist nurses.

## End of life planning

The majority of COPD patients die with exacerbations. This makes it difficult to predict when they will die. Their health status will vary during severe exacerbations and it is difficult to judge the likely level of recovery. Symptom scores do not predict the outcome for any individual. Most will die in hospital and some will have ventilatory support. As they deteriorate, patients, or more likely their relatives, could be asked if it is time to withhold or withdraw treatment. A recent US survey found that the biggest fear for patients with severe disease was that of being kept alive for too long, using life support.

These decisions are much easier to reach if the situation has been discussed before, especially if written directions are available. The decision about active resuscitation is useful to avoid unnecessary trauma to patients and their families; however, it should only be made in the context of a wider discussion of treatment options.

### Advanced directives/living wills

Patients might wish to make either an advanced directive or a living will, and if this is the case then their wishes should be respected and the documentation made available in all relevant notes.

### Place of death

Guidelines indicate that COPD should be managed at home unless the patient requires intensive nursing care or the patient and/or carer cannot cope. For many patients, respite care in a hospice would be a boon, and for some with steady deterioration this is an appropriate setting. Given the need for oxygen and intensive nursing care, few patients are supported enough to be able to die at home.

### Social/family support

The losses that afflict patients also affect their families. Spouses lose their social life, pleasurable activities such as travel, eating out and seeing their relatives. They become burdened by nursing care and take responsibilities for decisions about treatment – *'Shall we call the doctor?'* *'Shall we start steroid pills?'* Unless armed with a plan of action they feel helpless when their loved-one deteriorates. They are there for their spouse, but who is there for them? Their burdens can be eased greatly by involving them in frank discussions, obtaining maximum social and financial support. Relationships can suffer as a patient deteriorates, at the very time when a strong relationship might ease the burden of disease.

There appears to be very little correlation between physiological and psychological functioning. An important part of the care of patients should include addressing the psychological and social factors that can affect patients (*see Table 27*).

## Treatment of specific issues

### Dyspnoea

This is the overriding symptom for most patients. In the terminal phase, opiates have been shown to be effective. Codeine (30 mg 3-times a day) can reduce breathlessness and is also useful in cough. Using morphine in slow-release tablets (20 mg daily) is effective at reducing dyspnoea and aiding sleep. It can be considered relatively safe but can cause some side-effects, particularly constipation. Clearly respiratory depression is a consideration that should be discussed with both patient and relatives, but it should not be seen as a problem in patients in the dying phase. Some practitioners might worry about addiction, but for patients with a chronic progressive disease it is probably of little consequence.

### Anxiety and depression

These are almost always present. Relaxation and breathing exercises are very helpful to many patients who, in their anxiety, tend to hyperventilate and decrease alveolar ventilation by fast, shallow breathing patterns. Patients can also be taught to effectively clear their sputum.

**Table 27.** The aims of psychosocial support

Minimise the impact of the patients' disease on their lifestyle.

Maximise the patients' potential.

Encourage independence.

Give support and reinforce the patients' own coping mechanisms.

Allow for a degree of optimism and hope.

Encourage the patient to use anxiety and panic management techniques.

Anxiety and depression are amenable to antidepressants. Tricyclic antidepressants have anticholinergic effects and cause sedation, both of which can be of benefit to selected patients. Buspirone is also of value in reducing anxiety and depression in COPD. On the whole, psychotropic medication is under-used in severe COPD, especially given the high levels of anxiety and depression.

## Pain

Chest pains might be a result of respiratory muscle hypoxia, and musculoskeletal problems are generally common in inactive elderly populations. The full range of analgesics can be used, but are often overlooked. Codeine can be useful both for pain and for reducing the sensation of breathlessness, although the side-effect of constipation might deter some patients.

# Respiratory failure

## Oxygen, nebulisers and NIV

COPD is a progressive disease, and as respiratory function diminishes the levels of oxygen in blood can fall. This increases breathlessness and also initiates changes in the pulmonary circulation leading to pulmonary hypertension and *cor pulmonale*. If oxygen can be maintained at near-normal levels for at least 16 hours a day, the changes to the pulmonary system do not occur and mortality can be reduced significantly. Long-term oxygen therapy is the only treatment shown to prolong life in COPD.

Pulse oximetry is simple to perform in the patient's home and oxygen saturations of < 92% indicate a need for assessment for oxygen treatment, which should usually be carried out in hospital. Short burst oxygen is often prescribed wrongly or inappropriately, but in the terminal phase oxygen can provide symptomatic relief.

The use of oxygen should be clearly explained to patients. It can be delivered by nasal cannulae or mask. Nasal cannulae can facilitate eating and drinking without the claustrophobic effect of a mask, although the decision of which to use is often down to patient preference. Some patients may feel benefit from a cylinder of oxygen for use after exercise especially if they desaturate, although there is little evidence to substantiate this use.

Nebulisers may have a place in the palliation of symptoms for patients. Higher doses of bronchodilators can be given, and, in some patients, normal saline may help with expectoration and cough. There is also a large psychological element to using a nebuliser and patients might appreciate the cooling effect on the facial sensory receptors. Nebulised lignocaine can be useful for cough but should only be used under specialist (consultant) guidance.

Non-invasive ventilation (NIV) is effective in treating hypercapnic patients in an acute inpatient population, although there are some current trials of home NIV.

## Conclusions

Patients with COPD have a progressive incurable disease and have needs which are essentially palliative in nature. Quality, rather than quantity, of life is important. In general there has been a lack of recognition of the burden that COPD places both on the individual and on health care resources. Good terminal care requires understanding of the patients' perceptions, their overt problems and hidden fears. They need information from a trusted source and support from a multi-disciplinary team. The message that nothing more can be done is inappropriate, as there is always something that can be done for the patient and their family.

## What could I do?

■ Encourage palliative care services to widen their remit to include care to all patients with terminal disease, including those with COPD.

■ Regularly measure and record patient's weight, and therefore BMI, as a marker of prognosis and well-being.

■ Remember the importance of exacerbations – most patients with COPD will die during an exacerbation, or might not recover full health status.

■ Recognise COPD patients' feelings of guilt, fear, anxiety and social isolation.

■ Encourage all health care professionals to take time to talk – to identify and assess the patient's concerns; deal with their agenda.

■ Consider end of life planning, advanced directives and living wills.

■ Be aware of the needs of carers.

■ Ensure patients have access to a domiciliary oxygen service when appropriate.

# Further reading

Addington-Hall, J.M. and Higginson, I.J. (2001) *Palliative Care for Non-Cancer Patients*. Open University Press: Oxford.

American Thoracic Society (1999) Dyspnoea, mechanisms, assessment and management: a consensus statement. *Am. J. Respir. Crit. Care Med.*, **159**:321–340.

Barnes, P.J. (1999) *Managing Chronic Obstructive Pulmonary Disease*. Science Press.

British Thoracic Society Guidelines for the management of Chronic Obstructive Pulmonary Disease (1997). The COPD Guidelines Group of the Standards of Care Committee of the BTS. *Thorax*, **52**(suppl 5):S1–S32.

British Thoracic Society (2002) *The Burden of Lung Disease*. http://www.brit-thoracic.org.uk/pdf/BTS pages

Gore, J.M., Brophy, C.J. and Greenstone, M.A. (2000) How well do we care for patients with end stage chronic obstructive pulmonary disease (COPD)? A comparison of palliative care and quality of life in COPD and lung cancer. *Thorax*, **55**:1000–1006.

Health Media Group Medical Writer (2002) Understanding the treatment preferences of seriously ill patients. *New Engl. J. Med.*, **346**:1061–1066

Hill, K.M. and Meurs, M.F. (2000) Palliative care for patients with non-malignant end-stage respiratory disease. *Thorax*, **55**:979–981.

Jennings, A.L., Davies, A.N., Higgins, J.P., Gibbs, J.S. and Broadley, K.E. (2002) A systematic review of the use of opioids in the management of dyspnoea. *Thorax*, **57**:939–944.

Karajgi, B.R., Rifkin, A., Doddi, S. and Kelli, R. (1990) The prevalence of anxiety disorders in patients with chronic obstructive pulmonary disease. *Am. J. Psychiatry*, **147**:200–201

Keele-Card, G., Foxhall, M.J. and Barro, C.R. (1993) Loneliness, depression and social support of patients with COPD and their spouses. *Public Health Nurs.*, **10**:245–251.

Meurs, M.F. (2002) Opioids for dyspnoea. *Thorax*, **57**:922–923.

O'Driscoll, B.R. (1997) Nebulisers for chronic obstructive pulmonary disease. *Thorax*, **52**(suppl 2):S49–S52.

Schade, E. (2000) Risk of depression in patients with chronic obstructive pulmonary disease and its determinants. *Thorax*, **57**:412–416.

Simonds, A.K. (2003) Ethics and decision making in end-stage lung disease. *Thorax*, **58**:272–277.

# Chapter 15

## COPD and the new General
## Medical Services Contract
## for UK General Practice

**In this chapter:**

A new contract describing the terms and conditions, and remuneration of UK GPs was introduced in the UK in April 2004.

COPD is included as a clinical area in the quality and outcomes framework.

An accurate disease register and an IT system capable of recording and compiling data are essential to demonstrate performance.

In 2003, UK GPs voted to agree to the introduction of a new contract to supply general medical services. Included in this contract is a quality and outcomes framework that rewards general practices financially for delivering clinical care according to defined criteria in ten disease areas. COPD is one of the areas selected for this method of remuneration.

Within each clinical domain of the quality and outcomes framework, points, and therefore money, are awarded for a percentage achievement between the minimum (25% of patients on a disease register) and the maximum (usually 70–90% of patients). This is considered the maximum practically achievable figure.

Respiratory disease in general, and COPD in particular, has recently been over-looked by policy makers as disease areas worthy of attention, in favour of others such as heart disease, cancer and mental health. These diseases have achieved a higher socio-political status, despite the huge burden of respiratory disease on the community and the health care system. The inclusion of both COPD and asthma is welcome, therefore, although the selection of some criteria would appear to be on the basis of 'easy to measure' rather than 'important to measure', and the quality markers (see Fig. 32) often focus on process rather than outcome.

It is probable that the inclusion of COPD as a contract issue will encourage clinicians to focus attention on the disease, and we believe that the care of patients with COPD is likely to extend beyond the narrow criteria of the Contract indicators.

Clinicians might feel that there is a benefit in considering respiratory disease as a whole; spirometry, for example, is mentioned as a diagnostic tool in both the asthma and COPD criteria sets. The ubiquitous 'asthma clinic' in UK general practices was probably more correctly an 'inhaler clinic'. Sufficient differences exist in the management of the two conditions, however, to make it necessary to ensure that all clinicians involved in the care of these patients have appropriate training in the management of both conditions. Disease registers may have been combined and, for the purposes of both achieving quality indicators and effective management of the separate conditions, will now need to be segregated. It is unlikely that practices without adequate information technology (IT) systems, i.e. computers, appropriate programmes and the staff trained to use them, will be able to demonstrate that they have successfully achieved the quality indicators.

**Figure 32.** GMS contract quality markers

| Indicator | Points | Maximum threshold |
|---|---|---|
| **RECORDS** | | |
| **COPD 1**<br>The practice can produce a register of patients with COPD | 5 | |
| **INITIAL DIAGNOSIS** | | |
| **COPD 2**<br>The percentage of patients where diagnosis has been confirmed by spirometry including reversibility testing for newly diagnosed patients w.e.f. 01/04/03. | 5 | 90% |
| **COPD 3**<br>The percentage of all patients with COPD where diagnosis has been confirmed by spirometry including reversibility testing. | 5 | 90% |
| **ONGOING MANAGEMENT** | | |
| **COPD 4**<br>The percentage of patients with COPD in whom there is a record of smoking status in the previous 15 months. | 6 | 90% |
| **COPD 5**<br>The percentage of patients with COPD who smoke, whose notes contain a record that smoking cessation advice has been offered in the past 15 months. | 6 | 90% |
| **COPD 6**<br>The percentage of patients with COPD with a record of FEV1 in the previous 27 months. | 6 | 70% |
| **COPD 7**<br>The percentage of patients with COPD receiving inhaled treatment in whom there is a record that inhaler technique has been checked in the preceding 2 years. | 6 | 90% |
| **COPD 8**<br>The percentage of patients with COPD who have had influenza immunisation in the preceding 1 September to 31 March. | 6 | 85% |

# Setting up a disease register for COPD

A prerequisite of addressing any disease area is an accurate, up-to-date disease register.

For practices that have used a disease coding system as part of their usual clinical practice, a COPD register can be compiled by searching by Read code. Some useful Read codes are given in *Table 28*. A search of H3, for example, should identify all patients with COPD and asthma. Excluding H33 will identify patients coded with obstructive airways disease and not asthma. A significant overlap in coding reflecting imprecise diagnosis or a less than completely accurate data entry and the existence of more than one code for each patient should be anticipated. All patients with a record of H33 (asthma) should ideally have the diagnosis confirmed, preferably by lung function testing including reversibility; no small task indeed. Additionally, a coded history of lung function testing can be searched for.

All patients, male and female, over 40 years with a significant smoking history, with multiple attendances with lower respiratory tract infections, cough or breathlessness should have a diagnosis of COPD considered.

**Table 28.** Read codes in obstructive lung disease

| Read Code | Description |
|-----------|-------------|
| H3 | COPD |
| H30 | Bronchitis unspecified |
| H31 | Chronic bronchitis |
| H32 | Emphysema |
| H33 | Asthma |
| H36 | Mild COPD |
| H37 | Moderate COPD |
| H38 | Severe COPD |
| H3y | Other specified chronic obstructive airways disease |
| H3z | Chronic obstructive airways disease NOS |

In the absence of a consistent methodological approach to Read coding, a search can be carried out using prescriptions for key treatments. It is unlikely that any patients with significant airways disease will not have been prescribed either an inhaled short-acting beta agonist or an anticholinergic. A search for these drugs, or indeed by BNF drug block (3.1.1.1 and 3.1.2), will identify all these patients. Diagnosis of COPD, asthma, or both, then requires individual case analysis by an appropriate clinician. *Table 29* below summarises the process of developing an accurate COPD register.

## Spirometry

Spirometry is the gold standard diagnostic test for COPD and is described in detail in Chapter 3. The Contract rewards the use of spirometry in making a diagnosis of COPD in two ways: the percentage of patients in whom diagnosis has been confirmed by spirometry, including reversibility testing for newly

**Table 29.** Summary of developing a COPD register

| |
|---|
| From existing register, check individual case records to establish that a diagnosis of COPD is secure. If there is diagnostic doubt, perform spirometry with reversibility testing. |
| From asthma register, identify those over 40 years with a substantial history of smoking ( > 20 pack years) and conduct spirometry with reversibility testing. |
| Conduct a practice computer treatment search: anticholinergics, including tiotropium, short-acting β-agonists, (BNF drug blocks 3.1.1.1 and 3.1.2), oral steroid courses. Refer those considered likely to have COPD from record review for spirometry with reversibility testing. |
| Opportunistic case finding: over time, identify asymptomatic smokers and perform spirometry with reversibility testing. |
| Consider others at risk: smokers with regular cough, morning sputum production and recurrent antibiotics for respiratory tract infections. |

diagnosed patients; and the percentage of all patients in whom the diagnosis has been confirmed by spirometry, again including reversibility testing. Realistically, it will be easier to achieve the points available for the first of these – conducting spirometry and (lack of) reversibility for newly diagnosed patients – as the numbers will be smaller and manageable. The source of the spirometry is unimportant and practices might be fortunate enough to have previous practice records or access to hospital or clinic spirometry results for many patients with diagnosed COPD. For the purposes of the Contract, a diagnosis of COPD is made if the $FEV_1/FVC$ ratio is $< 70\%$ (as is accepted in UK and international guidelines) but only if the $FEV_1$ is $< 70\%$. The nationally and internationally accepted figure for making a diagnosis of COPD is an $FEV_1 < 80\%$ (*see Appendix 1*). A pragmatic, if not consistent, view has been taken which is likely to offend the purist. Again for the purposes of the contract, there is no need to classify disease severity as described in national and international guidelines. The UK National Institute for Clinical Excellence (NICE) guideline on the management of COPD, published in February 2004, does not advocate the use routinely of spirometry + reversibility in the diagnosis of COPD. Many clinicians, particularly in primary care, disagree with this approach. The NICE statement conflicts with the GMS Contract Quality and Outcomes framework. At the time of going to press this matter remains unclear and unresolved.

## Annual review

Annual review can be conducted by any appropriately trained clinician and many general practices will agree responsibilities between GPs and appropriately trained nurses. The review should include:

- recording of smoking status

- the offer of smoking cessation advice or referral

- confirmation of influenza vaccine in the preceding
  1 September to 31 March.

**Additionally every 2 years:**

- an inhaler technique check;

**and every 3years:**

- FEV1

The preferred Read codes are listed in *Table 30*.

**Table 30.** Preferred Read codes for COPD GP new contract

| Disease register | COPD | H32 |
|---|---|---|
| Spirometry | Reversibility positive<br>Spirometry screening | 33G1*<br>68M |
| Smoking | Never smoked<br>Ex-smoker<br>Smoker<br>Smoking cessation advice | 1371<br>137L<br>137R<br>8CAL |
| Influenza vaccine | Given<br>Contraindicated | 65E<br>812F |
| Inhaler technique | Observed | 6637 |

*Code 33G1 refers to 'reversibility positive' and is, alone, unhelpful. The presence of reversibility is *against* a diagnosis of COPD. A code is required for 'reversibility testing performed and *negative*' (33G0). This is not currently offered as a preferred code. This list is not exhaustive. A full and agreed list of Read codes in primary care respiratory medicine is available on the GPIAG website (http://www.gpiag.org/forum/index.php). http://www.gpiag.org/forum/final_codes_mark_levys_respiratory_codes_04022004.xls

# Data collection systems

Most computer systems in UK general practice allow for the easy recording of Read codes. Many problems exist in searching, collating and reporting these data in a manageable, contract-friendly way. A number of commercial and administrative bodies are currently grappling with this problem.

An example of a data collection screen is given in *Fig. 33*. The authors of this tool have extended the data set to include items beyond the current Contract requirements but which are felt to enhance the quality of care.

**Figure 33.** Data collection screen

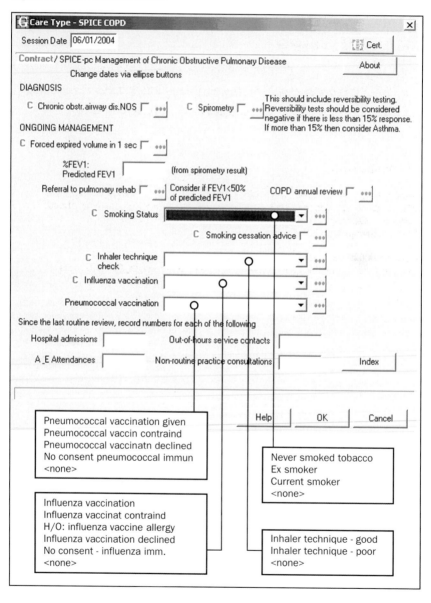

## What could I do?

- Compile a COPD register.
- Attempt to achieve as many New Contract points as possible.
- Expect some improvement in the well being of people with COPD.
- Anticipate an impact on the Practice prescribing drug budget.

## Further reading

New GMS Contract 2003 – Investing in General Practice. NHS Confederation, BMA.
NICE Guideline 12. National Clinical Guideline on management of chronic obstructive pulmonary disease in adults in primary and secondary care (2004)
*Thorax*, **59**(suppl 1):1–232.

Read codes for use in primary care respiratory medicine:
www.gpiag.org/forum/final_codes_mark_levys_respiratory_codes_04022004.xls

# Appendix I

**Guidelines on
Grading Severity
of COPD**

UK clinicians are faced, at first glance, with conflicting guidance on the grading of severity of COPD. It is probably useful to consider two cut-off points for severity, regardless of the differing descriptions given: $FEV_1$ < 50%, when pulmonary rehabilitation, long-term oxygen therapy and inhaled steroids (or inhaled steroid/long-acting β-agonist combinations) might be considered more strongly, and $FEV_1$ < 30%, which denotes serious airflow obstruction (*see below*)

**Disease severity according to FEV1 as a percentage of predicted value (NICE, 2004). FEV1/FVC < 0.7**

| Severity | FEV1 |
| --- | --- |
| Mild airflow obstruction | 50–80% predicted |
| Moderate airflow obstruction | 30–49% predicted |
| Severe airflow obstruction | <30% predicted |

**Disease severity according to FEV1 as a percentage of predicted value [Global Initiative for Chronic Obstructive Lung Disease (GOLD), 2004]**

(Chronic symptoms. Exposure to risk factors)

**FEV1/FVC < 0.7**

| Severity (grade) | | FEV1 |
| --- | --- | --- |
| 0 | at risk | Normal spirometry |
| I | Mild | ≥ 80% predicted |
| II | Moderate | 50–80% predicted |
| III | Severe | 30–50% predicted |
| IV | Very severe | < 30% predicted |

Definition of COPD, GMS contract (2004): FEV1/FVC < 0.7 and FEV1 < 70%

# Index